THE MOTHER

Pearl S. Buck

D0103660

MOYER BELL
Wakefield, Rhode Island & London

Published by Moyer Bell

Second Printing, 2000

LIBRARY OF CONGRESS
CATALOGING-IN-PUBLICATION DATA

Buck, Pearl S. (Pearl Sydenstricker), 1892-1973.
The mother / Pearl S. Buck.
        p.   cm.
1.Family—China—Fiction. I. Title.
PS3503.U198M6
                                1993
813'.52--dc20   93-13335
ISBN 1-55921-091-5 pb.   CIP

Cover illustration: *Former Consorts and Palace Ladies,*
Shanxi Provincial Museum

Printed in the United States of America.
Distributed in North America by Publishers Group West,
1700 Fourth Street, Berkeley, CA 94710, 800-788-3123 (in
California 510-528-1444); in Europe by Gazelle Book
Service, Falcon House, Queen Square, Lancaster LA1 1RN,
England; in Singapore by Horizon Books PTE Ltd.

THE

MOTHER

I

IN the kitchen of the small thatched farmhouse the mother sat on a low bamboo stool behind the earthen stove and fed grass deftly into the hole where a fire burned beneath the iron cauldron. The blaze was but just caught and she moved a twig here, a handful of leaves there, and thrust in a fresh bit of the dried grass she had cut from the hillsides last autumn. In the corner of the kitchen as near as she could creep to the fire sat a very old and weazened woman, wrapped in a thick padded coat of bright red cotton stuff, whose edges showed under a patched coat of blue she wore over it. She was half blind with a sore disease of the eyes, and this had well-nigh sealed her eyelids together. But through the small slits left open she could see a great deal still, and she watched the flare of the flames as they leaped and caught under the strong and skillful hands of the mother. Now she said, her words hissing softly through her sunken, toothless gums, "Be careful how you feed the fire—there is only that one load—is it two?— and the spring is but newly come and we have long to go before the grass is long enough to cut and here I am as

I am and I doubt I can ever go again and pick a bit of fuel—a useless old crone now, who ought to die—"

These last words the old woman said many times a day and every time she said them she waited to hear the son's wife speak as she now did, "Do not say it, old mother! What would we do if we had not you to watch the door while we are in the field and see that the little ones do not fall into the pond?"

The old mother coughed loudly at this and gasped out of the midst of her coughing, "It is true—I do that—the door must be watched in these evil times with thieves and robbers everywhere. If they came here, such a screeching as I would raise, daughter! Well I mind it was not so when I was young—no, then if you left a hoe out in the night it was there at dawn and in summer we tied the beast to the door hasp outside and there it stood again the next day and—"

But the young mother although she laughed dutifully and called out, "Did you, then, old mother!" did not hear the old woman, who talked incessantly throughout the day. No, while the old cracked voice rambled on the young mother thought of the fuel and wondered indeed if it would last until this spring planting were finished when she could take time to go out with her knife and cut small branches from trees and pick up this bit and that. It was true that just outside the door of the kitchen at the edge of the threshing-floor, which was also door-yard, there were still two ricks of rice straw, neatly rounded and roofed with hard packed clay to shield them from the damps of rains and snow. But rice straw was too good to burn. Only city folk burned rice straw, and she or her man would carry it into the city in great bundles upon a pole and gain good silver for it. No, rice straw could not be burned except in city houses.

She fed the grass into the stove bit by bit, absorbed in the task, the firelight falling on her face, a broad, strong face, full lips, and darkly brown and red with wind and sun. Her black eyes were shining in the light, very clear eyes, set straight beneath her brows. It was a face not beautiful but passionate and good. One would say, here is a quick-tempered woman but warm wife and mother and kind to an old woman in her house.

The old woman chattered on. She was alone all day except for the little children since her son and son's wife must labor on the land, and now it seemed there were many things she had to tell this daughter-in-law whom she loved. Her old wheezing voice went on, pausing to cough now and again in the smoke which poured out of the stove. "I ever did say that when a man is hungered and especially a young and hearty son like mine, an egg stirred into noodles—" The old voice lifted itself somewhat higher against the fretting of two children who clung to their mother's shoulders as she stooped to feed the fire.

But the mother went steadily on with her task, her face quiet and in repose. Yes, she was as quiet as though she did not hear the fretting of the children, this boy and this girl, and as though she did not hear the endless old voice. She was thinking that it was true she was a little late tonight. There was a deal to be done on the land in the spring, and she had stayed to drop the last row of beans. These warm days and these soft damp nights, filled with dew—one must make the most of them, and so she had covered the last row. This very night life would begin to stir in those dry beans. This thought gave her content. Yes, that whole field would begin to stir with life tonight secretly in the damp warm earth. The man was working there still, pressing the earth tight over the rows with his bare feet. She had left him there because over the fields came the voices of the children crying her name, and she had hastened and come home.

The children were standing hungrily at the kitchen door when she reached there and they were both weeping, the boy gently and steadily, his eyes tearless, and the little girl whimpering and chewing her fist. The old woman sat listening to them serenely. She had coaxed them for a time but now they were beyond her coaxing and would not be comforted and so she let them be. But the mother said nothing to them. She went swiftly to the stove, stooping to pick up a load of fuel as she went. Yet this was sign enough. The boy ceased his howling and ran after her with all the speed of his five years, and the girl came after as best she could, being but three and a little less.

THE MOTHER

Now the food in the cauldron was boiling and from under the wooden lid clouds of fragrant steam began to creep forth. The old woman drew deep breaths and champed her empty old jaws a little. Under the cauldron the flames leaped high and beat against its iron bottom and finding no vent they spread and flew out again, changing into dense smoke that poured into the small room. The mother drew back and pulled the little girl back also. But the acrid smoke had already caught the child and she blinked and rubbed her eyes with her grimy fists and began to scream. Then the mother rose in her quick firm way and she lifted the child and set her outside the kitchen door, saying, "Stay there, small thing! Ever the smoke hurts your eyes and ever you will thrust your head into it just the same."

The old woman listened as she always did whenever her son's wife spoke, and she took it as a fresh theme for something to say herself. Now she began, "Aye, and I always said that if I had not had to feed the fire for so many years I would not be half blind now. Smoke it was that made me be so blind as I am now and smoke—"

But the mother did not hear the old voice. She heard the sound of the little girl as she sat there flat upon the earth, screaming and rubbing her eyes and essaying to open them. It was true the child's eyes were always red and sore. Yet if anyone said to the mother, "Has not your child something amiss with her eyes?" the mother answered, "It is only that she will thrust her head into the fiery smoke when I am burning the grass in the oven."

But this crying did not move her as once it had. She was too busy now, and children came thick and fast. When her first son had been born, she could not bear to hear him cry at all. Then it had seemed to her that when a child cried a mother ought to still it somehow and give it ease, and so when the child wept she stopped whatever she did and gave him her breast. Then the man grew angry because she stopped so often at her share of the work, and he roared at her, "What—shall you do thus and leave it all to me? Here be you, but just begun your bearing and for these next twenty years shall you be suckling one or another, and am I to bear this? You are no rich man's wife who needs do naught but bear and suckle and can hire the labor done!"

She flew back at him then as ever she did, for they were both young and full of temper and passion, and she cried at him, "And shall I not have a little something for my pains? Do you go loaded many months to your work as I must do, and do you have the pains of birth? No, when you come home you rest, but when I go home there is the food to cook and a child to care for and an old woman to coax and coddle and tend for this and that—"

So they quarreled heartily for a while and neither was the victor and neither vanquished, they were so well matched. But still this one quarrel did not need to last long; her breasts soon went dry, for she conceived as easily as a sound and cleanly beast does. Even now was her milk dry again, though one child she dropped too soon last summer when she fell and caught herself upon the point of the plough. . . . Well, children must make shift now as best they could, and if they wept they must weep, and it was true that she could not run to give them suck, and they must wait and suit their hunger to her coming. So she said, but the truth was her heart was softer than her speech, and she still made haste if her children called to her.

When the cauldron boiled a while and the smoke was mingled with the smell of the fragrant rice, she went and found a bowl and first she poured it full for the old woman. She set it on the table in the larger room where they all lived, and then she led her there, scarcely heeding her gabbling voice, "—and if you mix pease with the rice it does make such a fine full taste as ever was—" And the old woman seated herself and seized the bowl in her two chill dry hands and fell silent, suddenly trembling with greediness for the food, so that the water ran from the corners of her wrinkled mouth, and she fretted, "Where is the spoon—I cannot find my spoon—"

The mother put the porcelain spoon into the fumbling old hand and she went out and this time she found two small tin bowls and filled them and she found two small pairs of bamboo chopsticks, and she took one bowl to the girl first because she was still weeping and rubbing her eyes. The child sat in the dust of the threshing-floor, and what with her tears and what with her grimy fists, her face was caked with mud and tears. Now the mother lifted her to her feet and wiped her face somewhat with the palm of her rough dark hand, and then lifting the edge of the patched coat the child wore, she wiped her eyes. But she was gentle enough, for it was true the child's eyes were red and tender and the edges of the lids turned out and raw, and when the child turned her head wincing and whimpering, the mother let be in pity, troubled for the moment with the child's pain. She set the bowl then upon a rude and unpainted table that stood outside the door of the house and she said to the child in her loud, kind voice, "Come—eat!"

The girl went unsteadily and stood clinging to the table, her red-rimmed eyes half closed against the piercing gold of the evening sun, and then stretched her hands toward the bowl. The mother cried, "Take heed—it is hot!"

And the girl hesitated and began to blow her little shallow breaths upon the food to cool it. But the mother continued to gaze upon her, still troubled as she gazed, and she muttered to herself, "When he takes that next load of rice straw to the city I will ask him to go to a medicine shop and buy some balm for sore eyes."

Now the boy was complaining because she had not set his bowl down on the table, too, and so she went and fetched it and set it down and for a time there was silence.

Then the mother felt herself too weary for a while even to eat and she gave a great sigh and went and fetched the little bamboo stool and set it by the door and sat down to rest. She drew in her breath deeply and smoothed back her rough sun-browned hair with her two hands and looked about her. The low hills that circled about this valley where their land lay grew slowly black against a pale yellow sky, and in the heart of this valley, in the small hamlet, fires were lit for the evening meal and smoke began to rise languidly into the still windless air. The mother watched it and was filled with content. Of the six or seven houses which made up the hamlet there was not one, she thought suddenly, in which the mother did better for her children than did she for hers. Some there were who were richer; that wife of the innkeeper, doubtless, had some silver and to spare, for she wore two silver rings upon her hands and rings in her ears such as the young mother used to long for in her girlhood and never had. Well, even so, she had liefer see her own spare silver go into the good flesh the children wore upon their bones. The gossip said the innkeeper gave his children but the meats the guests left in their bowls. But the mother gave her own children good rice that they grew upon their land, and if the girl's eyes were well there would be nothing wrong with them at all; sound and well grown were they, and

the boy big enough for seven or eight. Yes, she had sound
children always, and if that one had not come too soon,
and died when it had breathed but once, it would have
been a fair boy by now, too, and trying to walk soon.

She sighed again. Well, here was this new one coming in a month or two, and it was enough to think
about. But she was glad. Yes, she was glad and best content when she was big with child and when she was full
with life. . . .

Someone came out of the door across the street of the
little hamlet, and out of the smoking doorway she could
see her husband's cousin's wife, and she called, "Ah, you
are cooking, too! I am but just finished!"

"Yes—yes—" came the other's voice, carelessly cheerful. "And I was just saying, I dare swear you are finished,
you are so forward with your work."

But the mother called back loudly and courteously,
"No—no—it is only that my children grow hungry be-
times!"

"Truly a very able, forward woman!" cried the cousin's
wife again and went within once more, carrying the
grass she had come to fetch. The mother sat on a while
in the evening twilight, her face half smiling. It was true
she could rightly be proud, proud of her own strength,
proud of her children, proud of that man of hers. But
even so there could not be peace for long. The boy thrust
his bowl suddenly before her, "M-ma, more!"

She rose then to fill it for him again, and when she

came out of the door the sun rested in a dip between the hills, on the edge of the very field where she had worked that day long. It rested there, caught seemingly for an instant between the hills, and hung motionless, huge and solidly gold, and then it went slipping slowly out of sight. Out of the immediate dusk she saw the man coming along a footpath, his hoe over his shoulder and caught under his raised arm as he came buttoning his coat. He walked light and lithe as a young male cat, and suddenly he broke into singing. He loved to sing, his voice high and quivering and clear, and many a song he knew, so that oftentimes upon a holiday he was asked to sing for all in the teashop and so pass the time away. He lowered his voice as he came to the house, and when at last he reached the threshold he was only singing a very little but still in that high, shaking, thrilling voice, his words set into some swift rhythm. He put his hoe against the wall, and the old woman, hearing him, woke out of a doze that had fallen on her after she had eaten and she began to speak as though she had not left off, "As I said, my son likes a little pease mixed in his rice and such a full sweet taste—"

The man laughed an easy idle laugh and went into the house, and out of the door his pleasant voice came, "Aye, old mother, and so I do!"

Outside the door the girl child, her bowl emptied, sat passive and filled and now that the sun was gone she opened her eyes a little and looked about her more easily

and without complaining. The mother went into the
kitchen again and brought out a steaming bowl of rice
for the man. It was a large bowl of coarse blue and white
pottery, and it was filled to the brim. Into it the mother
had dropped an egg she had saved from the few fowls
they kept and now the fresh white of the egg began to
harden. When the man worked hard he must have a bit
of meat or an egg. However they might quarrel, it was
a pleasure to her to see him fed well, and all their quarreling, she thought to herself, was only of the lips. Well
she loved to see him eat, even if sometimes she belabored
him with her tongue for something. She called now to
the old woman, "I have put a new-laid egg into your
son's rice! And he has cabbage, too."

The old woman heard this and began instantly and
quickly, "Oh, aye—a new-laid egg! I ever did say a new-
laid egg—it is the best thing for a young man. It mends
the strength—"

But no one listened. The man ate hastily, being mightily hungered, and in no time he was calling for the
mother to fill his bowl again, thumping the table with
his empty bowl to hasten her. When it was filled she
went and fetched a bowl for herself. But she did not sit
down beside the man. She sat upon her low stool in the
dooryard and supped her rice with pleasure, for she loved
her food as a healthy beast does. Now and again she
rose to fetch a bit of cabbage from the man's bowl, and
as she ate she stared into the dark red sky between the

two hills. The children came and leaned upon her and held up their mouths to be fed and often the mother put a bit between their lips with her chopsticks. And although they were filled and no longer hungry, and although it was what they had eaten, yet this food from their mother's bowl seemed better to them than what they had in their own. Even the yellow farmyard dog came near with confidence. He had been sitting in hope under the table, but the man kicked him, and he slunk out and caught deftly the bits of rice the mother threw him once or twice.

Thrice the mother rose and filled the man's bowl and he ate to repletion and gave a grunt of satisfaction and then into his empty bowl she poured boiling water and he supped it loudly, rising now and supping as he stood outside the door. When he was through and she had taken his bowl he stood there a while, looking over the countryside as the night covered it. There was a young spring moon in the sky, very small and crystal pale among the stars. He stared at it and fell to singing some soft twisting song as he stood.

Out of the other few houses in the hamlet men began to come now also. Some shouted to each other of a game they had begun at the inn, and some stood yawning and gaping at their doors. The young husband ceased his singing suddenly and looked sharply across the street. There was only one house where a man worked on while others rested. It was his cousin. That fellow! He would work on even into the night. There he was sitting at his door, his head bent to see the weaving of a basket of some sort he made from willow withes. Well, some men were so, but as for himself—a little game—he turned to speak to the woman and met her hostile knowing look, and meeting it he cursed her silently. If he had worked all day, could he not game a bit at night either? Was he to work and work his life away? But he could not meet that steadfast, angry look upon him. He shook himself petulantly as a child does and he said, "After such a day of work as this—well, I will sleep then! I am too weary to game tonight!"

He went into the house then and threw himself upon the bed and stretched and yawned. His old mother, sightless in the dusk of the lampless room, called out suddenly, "Has my son gone to bed?"

"Aye, mother!" he answered angrily. "And what else is there to do in such a little empty place as this—work and sleep—work and sleep—"

"Yes, yes, work and sleep," the old woman answered cheerfully, hearing nothing of the anger in his voice, and she rose and felt her way to her own corner where behind a blue cotton curtain her pallet was. But the man was already asleep.

When she heard the sound of his breathing the mother rose, and the children followed, clinging to her coat. She rinsed the bowls with a little cold water from the jar that stood there by the kitchen door, and set them

22

in a cranny of the earthen wall. Then she went behind the house, and in the dim light of the moon she lowered a wooden bucket into a shallow well and dipped it full and took it to the jar and filled it. Once more she went out and this time to untie the water buffalo that stood tethered to one of the willow trees which grew raggedly about the threshing-floor, and she fed it straw and a few black pease with the straw. When the beast had eaten she led it into the house and tied it to the post of the bed where the man slept. The fowls were already roosting beneath the bed, and they cackled drowsily at her coming and fell silent again.

Once more she went out and called and a pig grunted out of the gathering darkness. She had fed it at noon and she did not feed it now, but pushing and prodding it gently she forced it into the house. Only the yellow dog she left for it must lie across the threshold.

All the time the two children had followed her as best they could, although she moved as she would without stopping for them. Now they clung to her trousered legs, whimpering and crying. She stooped and lifted the younger one into her arms, and leading the older by the hand, she took them into the house and barred the door fast. Then she went to the bed and laid the children at the man's feet. Softly she removed their outer garments and then her own, and creeping between the man and his children, she stretched herself out and drew the quilt over them all. There she lay stretched and still, her

23

strong body full of healthy weariness. Lying like this in the darkness she was filled with tenderness. However impatient she might be in the day, however filled with little sudden angers, at night she was all tenderness— passionate tenderness to the man when he turned to her in need, tender to the children as they lay helpless in sleep, tender to the old woman if she coughed in the night and rising to fetch a little water for her, tender even to the beasts if they stirred and frightened each other with their own stirring, and she called out to them, "Be still,—sleep—day is a long way off yet—" and hearing her rough kind voice even they were quieted and slept again.

Now in the darkness the boy nuzzled against her, fumbling at her breast. She let him suckle, lying in warm drowsiness. Her breast was dry, but it was soft and gave remembered comfort to the child. Soon it would be full again. Beyond the boy the girl lay, screwing her eyes tightly shut, rubbing at their incessant itching as she fell asleep. Even after she slept she tore at her eyes, not knowing what she did.

But soon they all slept. Heavily and deeply they all slept, and if the dog barked in the night they all slept on except the mother, for to them these were the sounds of the night. Only the mother woke to listen and take heed and if she needed not to rise, she slept again, too.

II

IS there one day different from another under heaven
for a mother? In the morning the mother woke
and rose before dawn, and while the others still
slept she opened the door and let out the fowls and the
pig and led the water buffalo into the dooryard, and she
swept up what filth they had dropped in the night and
put it upon the pile at a corner of the dooryard. While
the others still lay she went into the kitchen and lit the
fire and made water hot for the man and for the old
woman to drink when they woke, and some she poured
into a wooden basin to cool a little, so that she might
wash the girl's eyes.

Every morning the girl's eyes were sealed fast shut and
she could not see at all until they were washed. At first
the child had been frightened and so was the mother,
but the old grandmother piped, "So was I when I was
a child, and I never died of it!"

Now they were used to it and they knew it meant
nothing except that children could be so and not die of
it. Scarcely had the mother poured the water before the
children came, the boy leading the girl by the hand.
They had crept up silently and not waking the man,

fearing his anger, for with all his merry ways when he was minded to be merry, the man could be angry and cuff them furiously if he were waked before his sleep was ended. The two stood silently at the door and the boy winked his eyes with sleep and stared at his mother and yawned, but the little girl stood patiently waiting, her eyes sealed fast shut.

Then the mother rose quickly and taking the gray towel that hung upon a wooden peg driven into the wall she dipped the end of it into the basin and slowly wiped the girl's eyes. The child whimpered soundlessly and only with her breath, and the mother thought to herself as she thought every morning, "Well and I must see to the balm for this child's eyes. Some time or other I must see to it. If I do not forget it when that next load of rice straw is sold I will tell him to go to a medicine shop—there is one there by the gate to the right and down a small street—"

Even as she thought this the man came to the door drawing his garments about himself, yawning aloud and scratching his head. She said, speaking aloud her thought, "When you carry that load of rice straw in to sell do you go to that medicine shop that is by the Water Gate, and ask for a balm or some stuff for such sore eyes as these."

But the man was sour with sleep still and he answered pettishly, "And why should we use our scanty money for sore eyes when she can never die of it? I had sore eyes when I was a child, and my father never spent his money on me, though I was his only son who lived, too."

The mother, perceiving it was an ill time to speak, said no more, and she went and poured his water out. But she was somewhat angry too, and she would not give it to him but set it down on the table where he must reach for it. Nevertheless, she said nothing and for the time she put the matter from her. It was true that many children had sore eyes and they grew well as childhood passed, even as the man had, so that although his eyes were scarred somewhat about the lids as one could see who looked him full in the face, still he could see well enough if the thing were not too fine. It was not as though he was a scholar and had to peer at a book for his living.

Suddenly the old woman stirred and called out feebly, and the mother fetched a bowl of hot water and took it to her to sup before she rose, and the old woman supped it loudly, and belched up the evil winds from her inner emptiness and moaned a little with her age that made her weak in the morning.

The mother went back into the kitchen then and set about the morning food, and the children sat close together upon the ground waiting, huddled in the chill of the early morning. The boy rose at last and went to where his mother fed the fire, but the girl sat on alone. Suddenly the sun burst over the eastern hill and the light streamed in great bright rays over the land and these rays struck upon the child's eyes so that she closed them quickly. Once she would have cried out, but now she only drew her breath in hard as even a grown person might have done and sat still, her red eyelids pressed close together, nor did she move until she felt her mother push against her a bowl of food.

Yes, it is true that all days were the same for the mother, but she never felt them dull and she was well content with the round of the days. If any had asked her she would have made those bright black eyes of hers wide and said, "But the land changes from seedtime to harvest and there is the reaping of the harvest from our own land and the paying of the grain to the landlord from that land we rent, and there are the holidays of the festivals and of the new year, yes and even the children change and grow and I am busy bearing more, and to me there is naught but change, and change enough to make me work from dawn to dark, I swear."

If she had a bit of time there were other women in the hamlet and this woman due for birth and that one grieving because a child was dead, or one had a new pattern for the making of a flower upon a shoe, or some new way to cut a coat. And there were days when she went into the town with some grain or cabbage to sell, she and the man together, and there in the town were strange sights to see and think about if ever she had time to think at all. But the truth was that this woman was such

28

a one as could live well content with the man and children and think of nothing else at all. To her—to know the fullness of the man's frequent passion, to conceive by him and know life growing within her own body, to feel this new flesh take shape and grow, to give birth and feel a child's lips drink at her breast—these were enough. To rise at dawn and feed her house and tend the beasts, to sow the land and reap its fruit, to draw water at the well for drink, to spend days upon the hills reaping the wild grass and know the sun and wind upon her, these were enough. She relished all her life: giving birth, the labor on the land, eating and drinking and sleeping, sweeping and setting in rude order her house and hearing the women in the hamlet praise her for her skill in work and sewing; even quarreling with the man was good and set some edge upon their passion for each other. So therefore she rose to every day with zest.

On this day when the man had eaten and sighed and taken up his hoe and gone somewhat halting as he always did to the field, she rinsed the bowls and sat the old woman out in the warmth of the sun and bade the children play near but not go too near the pond. Then she took her own hoe and set forth, stopping once or twice to look back. The thin voice of the old woman carried faintly on the breeze and the mother smiled and went on. To watch the door was the sole thing the old woman could do and she did it proudly. Old and half blind as she was, yet she could see if anyone came near who should not and she could raise a cry. A troublesome old woman she was, and a very troublesome old care often, and worse than any child and more, because she grew wilful and could not be cuffed as a child could. Yet when the cousin's wife said one day, "A very good thing it will be for you, goodwife, when that old thing is dead, so old and blind and full of aches and pains and pettish with her food doubtless," the mother had replied in the mild way she had when she was secretly tender, "Yes, but a very good use still, too, to watch the door, and I hope she will live until the girl is bigger."

Yes, the mother never had it in her heart to be hard on an old woman like that. Women she had heard who boasted of how they waged war in a house against their mothers-in-law and how they would not bear the evil tempers of the elder women. But to this young mother the old woman seemed but another child of hers, childish and wanting this and that as children do, so that sometimes it seemed a weary thing to run hither and thither upon the hills in spring seeking some herb the old soul longed for, yet when one summer came and there was a fierce flux in the hamlet so that two strong men died and some women and many little children, and the old woman lay dying, or so it seemed, and so seemed that they bought the best coffin they could and set there ready, the young mother was truly glad when the old woman clung to her life and came back to it for a while longer. Yes, even though the hardy old creature had worn out two burial robes, the mother was glad to have her live. It was a joke in the whole hamlet to see how the old life hung on. The red coat the young mother had made to bury her in she wore under a blue coat, as it was the custom to do in these parts, until it was worn and gone and the old woman fretted and was ill at ease until the mother had made it new again, and now she wore this second one merrily and if any called out, "Are you still there then, old one?" she would pipe back gaily, "Aye, here I be and my good grave clothes on me! A-wearing them out, I be, and I cannot say how many more I can wear out!"

And the old soul chuckled to think how good a joke it was that she lived on and on and could not die.

Now, looking back, the mother smiled and caught the old woman's voice, "Rest your heart, good daughter —here am I to watch the door!"

Yes, she would miss this old soul when dead. Yet what use missing? Life came and went at the appointed hour, and against such appointment there was no avail.

Therefore the mother went her way tranquil.

III

WHEN the beans she had planted in the field were come to flower and the winds were full of their fragrance and when the valley was yellow with the blooming of the rape they grew for the oil they pressed from its seeds, the mother gave birth to her fourth child. There was no midwife for hire in that small hamlet as there might be in a city or town or even in a larger village, but women helped each other when the need came, and there were grandmothers to say what to do if aught went wrong and a child came perversely or if there was anything in a birth to astonish a young woman. But the mother was well made, not too small or slight, and loosely knit and supple in the thighs, and there was never anything wrong with her. Even when she had fallen and dropped her child too soon, she did it easily, and it was little to her save the pity of a child lost and her trouble for naught.

In her time she called upon their cousin's wife, and when the cousin's wife needed it, she did the same for her. So now upon a sweet and windy day in spring the woman felt her hour on her and she went across the field and set her hoe against the house and she called out to the house across the way and the cousin's wife came running, wiping her hands on her apron as she came, for she had been washing clothes at the pond's edge. This cousin's wife was a kindly, good woman, her face round and brown and her nostrils black and upturned above a big red mouth. She was a noisy, busy soul, talking the livelong day beside her silent man, and now she came bustling and laughing and shouting as she came, "Well, goodwife, I do ever say how good a thing it is that we do not come together. I have been watching you and wondering which would come first, you or I. But I am slower somehow this year than I thought to be, and you are bearing and I but just begun!"

Her voice came out big and loud when she said this, for it was her way, and women hearing called from other houses and they said gaily, "Your hour is it, goodwife? Well, luck then, and a son!" And one who was a widow and a gossip called out mournfully, "Aye, make the most of your man while you have him, for here be I, a good bearing woman too, and no man any more!"

But the mother answered nothing. She smiled a little, pale under the dust and the sweat upon her face and she went into the house. The old woman followed after chattering and laughing in her pleasure in the hour, and she said, "I ever said when my hour used to come, and you know I bore nine children in my time, daughter, and all good sound children until they died, and I ever said—"

THE MOTHER

But the mother did not hear. She took a little stool and sat down without speaking anything and smoothed the rough hair from her face with her two hands and her hands were wet with sweat—not the sweat of the fields, but this new sweat of pain. And she took up the edge of her coat and wiped her face, and she uncoiled her thick long hair and bound it fresh and firm. Then the pain caught her hard, and she bent over silently, waiting.

Beside her the old woman clacked on and the cousin's wife laughed at her, but when she saw the mother bend like this she ran and shut the door, and stood to wait. But suddenly there came a beating on the door and it was the boy. He saw the door closed in the day and his mother inside and he was afraid and he set up a cry and would have the door opened. At first the mother said, "Let him be there so that I may have peace at this task," and the cousin's wife went to the door and bawled through the crack, "Stay there for a while for your mother is at her task!" And the old woman echoed, "Stay there, my little one, and I will give you a penny to buy peanuts if you will play well and you shall see what your mother will have for you in a little while!"

But the boy was afraid to see the door shut in the day-time and would have his way, and the girl began to whimper too as she did when her brother cried and she came feeling her way and beat too upon the door with her puny fists, and at last the mother grew angry in her pain and the more angry because it bore her down so

35

hard, and she rose and rushed out and cuffed the boy heartily and shouted at him, "Yes, and you do wear my life away and you never heed a thing that is said, and here is another to come just like you, I do swear!"

But the instant she had beat him her heart grew soft and the anger in her was satisfied and went out of her and she said more gently, "But there, come in if you must, and it is nothing to see, either." And she said to the cousin's wife, "Leave the door a little open, for they feel shut out from me, and they are not used to it."

Then she sat down again and held her head in her hands and gave herself silently to her pains. As for the boy, he came in and seeing nothing, but feeling his father's cousin's wife look at him hard as if he had done some ill thing, he went out again. But the little girl came in and sat down on the earthen floor beside her mother and held her hands against her eyes to ease them.

Thus they waited, the one woman in silence and in pain, and the other two talking of this and that in the hamlet and of the man in the farthest house and how today he was off gambling and his land lying there waiting for him, and how this morning the man and his wife had had a mighty quarrel for that he had taken the last bit of money in the house, and she, poor soul, had been no match for him, and when he was gone she had sat upon the doorstep and wailed out her woes for all to hear, and the cousin's wife said, "It is not as if he ever won a bit to bring home to her either. He can only lose and lose again, and this is what makes her so sorrowful." And the old woman sighed and spat upon the floor and said, "Aye, a very sorrowful thing it is when a man is made for losing and made so he never gains, but there be some men so, and well I know it, but not in my house, thank the gods, for my son is very good at winning in a game."

But before she had finished speaking the mother cried out and turned herself away a little from the girl and she loosened her girdle and leaned forward upon the stool. Then did the cousin's wife run forward and she caught nimbly in her two hands that little child for whom they waited, and it was a son.

As for the mother, she went and laid herself upon the bed and rested after her labor, and rest was sweet and she slept heavily and long. While she slept the cousin's wife washed and wrapped the child and laid him down beside the sleeping mother and she did not wake even when his little squeaking cry rang out. The cousin's wife went home then to her work once more and she bade the old woman send the boy to call her when the mother woke.

When the lad came crying, "Did you know I have a brother now?" she came quickly with a bowl of soup, laughing at the boy and teasing him and saying, "I brought the boy myself and do I not know?"

But the boy stared thoughtful at this and at last he said, "Is it not ours then to keep?" and the women

37

laughed, but the old woman laughed loudest of all, because she thought the boy so clever. The mother drank
the soup then gratefully, and she murmured to her
cousin's wife, "It is your good heart, my sister."

But the cousin's wife said, "Do you not the same for
me in my hour?"

And so the two women felt themselves the more deeply
friends because of this hour common to them both and
that must come again and yet again.

IV

BUT there was the man. To him there was no change in time, no hope of any new thing day after day. Even in the coming of the children his wife loved there was no new thing, for to him they were born the same and one was like another and all were to be clothed and fed, and when they were grown they must be wed in their turn and once more children born and all was the same, each day like to another, and there was no new thing.

In this little hamlet so had he himself been born, and except to go to the small town which lay behind a curve of the hill upon the river's edge, he had never once seen anything new in any day he lived. When he rose in the morning there was this circle of low round hills set against this selfsame sky, and he went forth to labor until night, and when night was come there were these hills set against this sky and he went into the house where he had been born and he slept upon the bed where he had slept with his own parents until it grew shameful and then they had a pallet made for him.

Yes, and now he slept there in the bed with his own wife and children and his old mother slept on the pallet, and it was the same bed and the same house, and even in the house scarcely one new thing except the few small things that had been bought at the time of his wedding, a new teapot, the blue quilt upon the bed newly covered, new candlesticks and a new god of paper on the wall. It was a god of wealth, and a merry old man he was made to be, his robes all red and blue and yellow, but he had never brought wealth to this house. No, this man looked often at the god and cursed him in his heart because he could look so merrily down from the earthen wall and into this poor room that was always and ever as poor as it was.

Sometimes when the man came home from a holiday in town or when he had gone on a rainy day to the little inn and gambled a while with the idlers there, when he came home again to this small house, to this woman bearing her children that he must labor to feed, it fell upon him like a terror that so long as he lived there was naught for him but this, to rise in the morning and go to this land of which they owned but little and rented from a landlord who lived in pleasure in some far city; to spend his day upon that rented land even as his father had done before him; to come home to eat his same coarse food and never the best the land could give, for the best must ever be sold for others to eat; to sleep, to rise again to the same next day. Even the harvests were not his own, for he must measure out a share to that landlord and he must take another share and fee the townsman who was the landlord's agent. When he thought of this agent he could not bear it, for this townsman was such a one as he himself would fain have been, dressed in soft silk and his skin pale and fair and with that smooth oily look that townsmen have who work at some small, light task and are well fed.

On such days when all these thoughts pressed on him he was very surly and he spoke not at all to the woman except to curse her for some slowness, and when her quick temper rose against him it was a strange malicious pleasure to him to fall to loud quarreling with her, and it eased him somehow, although she had often the best of him, too, because her temper was more stout than his, except when she was angry at a child. Even to his anger he could not cling as long as she did, but grew weary of it and flung himself off to something else. Quickest of all would her anger rise if he struck one of the children or shouted at one if it cried. Then she could not bear it, and she flew against him if it were to save a child and ever the child was right and he was wrong, and this angered him more than anything, that she put the children before him, or he thought she did.

Yes, on days like this he held as nothing even the good few holidays he took, the feast days and the long idle winter days when he did nothing but sleep, and when he could not sleep he gambled. A lucky gambler he was, too, and he always came home with more than he took, and it seemed an easy way to live, if he were a lone man and had but himself to feed. He loved the chance of gambling and the excitement and the merriment of the game and all the men crowded together to see what lucky play he made. Truly luck was in his nimble fingers, which even the plough and the hoe had not made stiff, for he was young yet, only twenty and eight years of age, and he had never worked more than he must.

But the mother never knew what was in the heart of the father of her children. That he loved play she knew, but what matter that if he did not lose at play? It was in truth a pride to her that when other women complained aloud of their own men and how the scanty earnings of the land were lost at that table in the inn, she need not complain, and when one cried out to her, "If my poor wretch were but like that pretty man of yours, goodwife, his fingers are faery somehow, so that the money crawls to them of its own accord, seemingly, upon the gaming table—a very lucky woman be you, goodwife!" she smiled complacently and she did not often blame him for his play unless it served as excuse for some other cause of quarrel.

And she did not blame him deeply that he could not work steadily hour after hour in the fields as she did, though at the moment she might lay about him sharply with her tongue. She knew that men cannot work as women do, but have the hearts of children always in them, and she was used now to working on in her steady way while he flung down his hoe and laid himself upon the grass that grew on the footpath between this field and the next and slept an hour or two. But when she said aught to him in her scolding way, which was but the way, after all, her tongue was used to speak, for secretly she loved him well, he would answer, "Yes, and sleep I may for I have worked enough to feed myself."

She might have said, "Have we not the children then and shall not each do what he is able to make more for them?" But this she did not say because it was true the children seemed ever hers and hers alone, since he did nothing for them. Besides, her tongue was not so adroit as his to find an answer.

But sometimes her wrath would come up hotly and then it would come with more than her usual scolding speech. Once or twice in a season a quarrel would go deep with her and give an unused bitterness to her tongue. When the man bought some foolish trinket in the market with the silver he had taken for the cabbage there, or when he was drunken on a day that was not a holiday, then she would grow angry and well-nigh she forgot she loved him in her heart. This was a deep fierce anger too, which smouldered and broke forth so many hours after his misdeed that the man had almost forgot what he had done, for it was his way to forget easily anything that did not please him, and when her anger came up in her like this she was helpless against it and it must out.

On such a day one autumn he came home with a gold

ring on his finger, or one he said was gold, and when she saw it her anger came up and she cried in the strangest, hottest way, "You—and you will not take your share of our common bitterness of life! No, you must needs go and spend the scant bit we have for a silly ring to put upon your little finger! And whoever heard of a good and honest poor man who wore a ring upon his finger? A rich man, he may do it and nothing said, but if a poor man does it, has it any good meaning? Gold! Whoever heard of a gold ring bought for copper?"

At this he shouted at her, his face rebellious as a child's, his red lips pouting, "It is gold, I tell you! It is stolen from some rich house, the man who sold it told me, and he showed it to me secretly upon the street as I passed, and he had it under his coat, and let me see it as I passed—"

But she sneered and said, "Yes, and what he saw was a silly countryman whom he could trick! And even though it were gold, what if it be seen upon your finger in the town some day and you be caught and thrown into a gaol for thief and then how will we buy you out again, or even feed you in the gaol? Give it to me and let me see if it be gold!"

But he would not give the toy to her. He shook himself sullenly as a child does and suddenly she could not bear him. No, she flew at him and scratched his smooth and pretty face and she beat him so heartily that he was aghast at her and he tore the ring from his finger scorn-

fully but half frightened, too, and he cried, "There—
take it! Very well I know you are angry because I bought
it for my own finger and not for yours!"

At this she felt fresh anger, because when he spoke
she was astonished to know he spoke the truth, and it
was secret pain to her that he never bought any trinket
to put into her ears or on her fingers as some men do
for their wives, and this she did think of when she saw
the ring. She stared at him and he said again, his voice
breaking with pity for himself and his hard life, "You
ever do begrudge me the smallest good thing for myself.
No, all we have must go for those brats you breed!"

He began to weep then in good earnest and he went
and flung himself upon the bed and lay there weeping
and making the most of his weeping for her to hear, and
his old mother who had heard the quarrel in greatest
fright ran to him as best she could and coaxed him lest
he be ill, and she cast hostile looks at the daughter-in-
law whom commonly she loved well enough, and the
children wept when they saw their father weep, and felt
their mother hard and harsh.

But the mother was not cool yet. She picked up the
ring from the dust where he had thrown it and put it
between her teeth and bit on it, lest by any chance it
might be the gold he said it was and a good bargain they
could sell again for something. It was true that sometimes stolen things were cheaply sold, but scarcely, she
thought, so cheaply as he said this was, although he

45

might have lied, perhaps, in fear of her. But when she bit on it the thing would not give at all between her hard white teeth as it must if the gold were pure, and she cried out in new anger, "And if it were gold would it not be soft between my teeth? It is brass and hard—" she gnawed at it a while and spat the yellow shallow gold from out her mouth— "See, it has scarce been dipped even in the gold!"

She could not bear it then that the man had been so childishly deceived, and she went out from him to work upon the land, her heart hard so that she would not see the sobbing children nor would she hear the old mother's quavering anxious voice that said, "When I was young I let my man be pleased—a wife should let her man be pleased with a little slight thing. . . ." No, she would not hear anything to cool her anger down.

But after she had worked a while on the land the gentle autumn wind blew into her angry heart and cooled it without her knowing it. Drifting leaves and brown hillsides from which the green of summer had died away, the gray sky and the far cry of wild geese flying southward, the quiescent land and all the quiet melancholy of the falling year stole into her heart without her knowledge and made her kind again. And while her hand scattered the winter wheat into the soft and well-tilled soil, in her heart came quiet and she remembered that she loved the man well and his laughing face came before her and stirred her and she said to herself remorsefully, "I will make him a dainty dish for his meal this noon. It may be I was too angry for but a little money spent, after all."

She was in great haste and longing to be gone then and at home to make the dish and show him she was changed, but when she was come there he still lay angry in the bed and he lay with his face inward and would not say a word. When she had made the dish and had caught some shrimps from the pond to mix into it as he liked and when she called him he would not rise and he would not eat at all. He said very faintly as though he were ill, "I cannot eat indeed—you have cursed the souls out of me."

She said no more then but set the bowl aside and went silent to her work again, her lips pressed hard together, nor would she aid the old mother when she besought her son to eat. But the mother could not beg him for she remembered freshly all her anger. And as she went the dog came up to her begging and hungry, and she went into the kitchen again and there the dish was she had made for the man. She put out her hand and muttered, "Well, then, I will even give it to the dog." But she could not do it. After all, it was food for men and not to be so wasted and she set the dish back in the niche of the wall and found a little stale cold rice and gave it to the dog. And she said to her heart that she was angry still.

Yet in the night when she laid herself beside him and the children curled against her in the darkness and she felt the man on her other side, her anger was clean gone. Then it seemed to her this man was but a child, too, and dependent on her as all in this house were, and when the morning came she rose, very gentle and quiet, and after all were fed except him, she went to him and coaxed him to rise and eat, and when he saw her like this he rose slowly as though from a sick bed and he ate a little of the dish she had made and then he finished it, for it was one he loved. And while he ate the old woman watched him lovingly, clacking as she watched, of this and that.

But he would not work that day. No, as the mother went out to the field he sat upon a stool in the sun of the doorway and he shook his head feebly and he said, "I feel a very weak place in me and a pain that flutters at the mouth of my heart and I will rest myself this day."

And the mother felt that she had been wrong to blame him so heartily that he was like this and so she said, soothing him and sorry for her anger, "Rest yourself, then," and went her way.

But when she was gone the man grew restless and he was weary of his mother's constant chatter, for the old woman grew very merry to think her son would be at home all day to talk to, though for the man it was a dull thing to sit and listen to her and see the children playing. He rose then, muttering he would be better if he had some hot tea in him, and he went down the little street to the wayside inn his fifth cousin kept. At the inn there were other men drinking tea, too, and talking, and tables were set under a canopy of cloth upon the street, where travelers might pass, and when such travelers stayed one heard a tale or two of this strange thing and that, and even perhaps some story-teller passed and told his tales, and indeed the inn was a merry, noisy place.

But as he went the man met his sober cousin coming from the field for his first morning meal, having already worked a space since dawn, and this cousin called, "Where do you go and not at work?"

And the man answered complaining and very weak, "That woman of mine has cursed me ill over some small thing I scarcely know, and there is no pleasing her, and she cursed me so sore I had an illness in the night and it frightened even her so that she bade me rest myself today and I go to drink a little hot tea for the comfort of my belly."

Then the cousin spat and passed on, saying nothing, for he was by nature a man who did not speak unless he must, and kept what few thoughts he had close in him.

So was the man impatient with his life and it seemed to him a thing not to be borne forever that there was to be no new thing for him, and only this wheel of days, year upon year, until he grew old and died. The more hard was it to him because the few travelers who came past the wayside inn told him of strange and wonderful things beyond the circle of the hills and at the mouth of the river that flowed past them. There the river met the sea, they said, and there was a vast city full of people of many hues of skin, and money was easy come by with very little work for it and gaming houses everywhere and pretty singing girls in every gaming house, such girls as the men in this hamlet had never even seen and could not hope to see their lives long. Strange sights there were in that city, streets as smooth as threshing-floors and carts of every sort, houses tall as mountains and shops with windows filled with merchandise of all the world that ships brought there from over seas. A man could spend a lifetime there looking at those windows and he could not finish with the looking. Good food and plenty was there, too, sea fish and sea meats, and after he had eaten a man might enter into a great playhouse where there was every sort of play and picture, some merry to make a man burst his belly with laughing and some strange and fierce and some very witty and vile to see. And strangest thing of all was this, that in the great city all the night was light as day with a sort of lamp they had, not made with hands nor lit with any flame, but with some pure light that was caught from out of heaven.

Sometimes the man gamed a while with such a traveler and ever the traveler was astonished at so skilled a gamester as he in this small country hamlet, and would cry, "Good fellow, you play as lucky as a city man, I swear, and you could play in any city pleasure house!"

The man smiled to hear this, then, and he said earnestly, "Do you think I could in truth?" and he would say in his own heart with scorn and longing, "It is true there is not one in this little dull place who dares play with me any more, and even in the town I hold my own against the townsmen."

When he thought of this more than ever did he long exceedingly to leave this life of his upon the land he hated and often he muttered to himself as his hoe rose and fell lagging over the clods, "Here I be, young and pretty and with my luck all in my fingers, and here I be, stuck like a fish in a well. All I can see is this round sky over my head and the same sky in rain or shine, and in my house the same woman and one child after another and all alike weeping and brawling and wanting to be fed. Why should I wear my good body to the bone to feed them and never find any merry thing at all for me in my own life?"

And indeed, when the mother had conceived and borne this last son he was even sullen and angered against her because she bore so easily and so quickly after the last birth, although very well he knew this is a thing for which a wife should be praised and not blamed, and he might complain with justice only if she were barren, but never if she bore in her due season every year and sons more often than not.

But in these days justice was not in him. He was but a lad still in some ways, and younger by some two years than his wife was, as the custom was in those parts, where it was held fitting for a man to be younger than his wife, and his heart rose hot and high within him and it was nothing to him that he was the father of sons, seeing that he longed for pleasure and strange sights and any idle joy that he could find in some city far away.

And indeed he was such a one as heaven had shaped for joy. He was well formed and not tall, but strong and slight and full of grace, his bones small and exquisite. He had a pretty face, too, his eyes bright and black and full of laughter at what time he was not sullen over something else, and when he was in good company he could always sing a new song of some kind and he had a quick and witty tongue, and he could say a thing seeming simple but full of wit and hidden coarseness such as the countrymen loved. He could set a whole crowd laughing with his songs and wit, and men and women too liked him very well. When he heard them laugh his heart leaped with pleasure in this power he had, and when he came home again and saw his wife's grave face and sturdy body it seemed to him that only she did not know him for the fine man he truly was, for only she never praised him. It was true he made no joke in his own house and he was seldom merry even with his own children. He was such a one as seemed to save all his good humor and his merry, lovable looks for strangers and for those who were not of his own house.

And the woman knew this, too, so that half it angered

her and half it was a pain when other women cried, "That man of yours, I do declare his tongue is good as any play, and his quick merry looks—"

And she would answer quietly, "Aye, a very merry man, truly," and would talk then of other things to hide her pain, because she loved him secretly. And she knew he was never merry when he was with her.

Now it happened that in the new summer time when the mother had borne her fourth child, the most evil quarrel that ever was between the man and woman came to pass. It was on a day in the sixth month of the year and it was early summer and it was such a day in that summer as might set any man to dreaming of new joy, and so that man had dreamed the whole morning long. The air was so full of languor and soft warmth, the leaves and grass so newly green, and the sky so bright and deep a blue that scarcely could he work at all. He could not sleep, either, for that day was too full of life for sleep, and the great heat not yet come. Even the birds made continual songs and chirping and there was a sweet wind, teasing and blowing now this fragrance and that down from the hill where yellow fragrant lilies bloomed and wild wistaria hung in pale purple wreaths. The wind blew against the sky, too, and shifted the great billowing clouds as white as snow, and they floated across the bright sky and set the hills and valley in such vivid light and darkness as are seldom seen, so that now it was bright and now shadowy, and there was no repose in the day. It was a day too merry for work, and very disturbing to the heart of any man.

In the noontime of that bright day it happened that a pedlar of summer stuffs came through the countryside, and he carried on his shoulder a great heap of his stuffs, of every hue and shade, and some were flowered, and as he went he called, "Cloth—good cloth for sale!"

When he came to this house where the man and the woman and the old mother and the little children sat in the shade of their willow tree and ate their noon meal he halted and cried, "Shall I stay, goodwife, and show you my stuffs?"

But the mother called back, "We have no money to buy, unless it be a foot of some common cheap stuff for this new son of mine. We be but poor farmer folk and not able to buy new clothes nor much of any stuffs except such as must be had to keep us from bareness!"

And the old woman, who must always put in her bit, cried in her little old shrill voice, "Aye, it is true what my daughter-in-law says, and the stuffs be very poor these days and washed to shreds in a time or two, and I mind when I was young I wore my grandmother's coat and it was good till I was married and needing something new but still only for pride's sake, for the coat was good enough still, but here I be in my second shroud and nearly ready for a third, the stuffs be so poor and weak these days—"

Then the pedlar came near, scenting sale, and he was a man with very pleasant and courteous coaxing ways such as pedlars have, and he humored the mother and had a good kindly word for the old woman, too, and he said to her, "Old mother, here I have a bit of cloth as good as any the ancients had and good enough even for that new grandson you have—goodwife, it is a bit left from a large piece that a rich lady bought in a great village I went through today, and she bought it for her only son. Of her I did ask the honest price seeing she cut from a whole piece, but since there is only this bit left, I will all but give it to you, goodwife, in honor of the fine new son you have there at your breast."

So saying these words smoothly and as though all in one flowing breath, the pedlar drew from out his pack a very pretty end of cloth, and it was as he said, flowered with great red peonies upon a grass-green ground.

The old woman cried out with pleasure because her dim eyes could see its hues so clear and bright, and the mother loved it when she saw it. She looked down then at the babe upon her breast, naked except for a bit of old rag about its belly, and it was true he was a fat and handsome child, the prettiest of her three, and like the father, and he would look most beautiful in that bit of flowery stuff. So it seemed to the mother and she felt her heart grow weak in her and she said unwillingly, "How much is that bit then? But still I cannot buy it for we have scarcely enough to feed these children and this old soul and pay the landlord too. We cannot buy such stuffs as rich women put upon their only sons."

The old woman looked very doleful at this, and the little girl had slipped from her place and went to peer at the bright cloth, putting her dim eyes near to see it. Only the elder lad ate on, caring nothing, and the man sat idly, singing a little, careless of this bit of stuff for no one but a child.

Then the pedlar dropped his voice low and coaxing and he held the cloth near the child, but not too near either, careful lest some soil come on it if it were not bought, and he said half whispering, "Such cloth—such strength—such color—I have had many a piece pass through my hands, but never such a piece as this. If I had a son of my own I would have saved it out for him, but I have only a poor barren wife who gives me no child at all, and why should the cloth be wasted on such as she?"

The old woman listened to this tale and when she heard him say his wife was barren she was vastly diverted and she cried out, "A pity, too, and you so good a man! And why do you not take a little wife, good man, and try again and see what you can do? I ever say a man must try three women before he knows the fault is his—"

But the mother did not hear. She sat musing and unsure, and her heart grew weaker still, for she looked down at her child and he was so beautiful with this fine new stuff against his soft golden skin and his red cheeks that she yielded and said, "What is your least price, then, for more I cannot pay?"

Then the pedlar named a sum, and it was not too high and not as high as she had feared, and her heart leaped secretly. But she shook her head and looked grave and named half the sum, as the custom was in bargaining in those parts. This was so little that the pedlar took the cloth back quickly and put it in its place and made to go away again, and then the mother, remembering her fair child, called out a sum a little more, and so haggling back and forth and after many false starts away the pedlar made, he threw down his pack again and pulled forth the bit, agreeing at last to somewhat less than he had asked, and so the mother rose to fetch the money from the cranny in the earthen wall where it was kept.

Now all this time the man sat idly by, singing, and his high voice made soft and small and stopping sometimes to sup down his hot water that he drank always after he had eaten, and he took no part in this bargain. But the pedlar being a very clever fellow and eager to turn to his account every passing moment, took care to spread out seemingly in carelessness a piece of grass cloth that he had, and it was that cloth made of wild flax which cools the flesh upon a hot day in summer, and in color it was like the sky, as clear, as blue. Then the pedlar glanced secretly at the man to see if the man saw it, and he said half laughing, "Have you bought a robe for yourself yet this summer? For if you have not, I have it for you here, and at a price I swear is cheaper than it can be bought in any shop in town."

But the man shook his head and a dark look came down upon his idle, pretty face, and he said with bitterness, "I have nothing wherewith to buy myself anything in this house. Work I have and nothing else, and all I gain for it is more to feed, the more I work."

Now the pedlar had passed through many a town and countryside and it was his trade to know men's faces and he saw at a glance that this man was one who loved his pleasure, and that he was like a lad held down to life he was not ready for, and so he said in seeming kindliness and pity, "It is true that I can see you have a very hard life and little gain, and from your fine looks I see it is too hard a life. But if you buy yourself a new robe you will find it like a very potent new medicine to put pleasure in your heart. There is nothing like a new summer robe to put joy in a man, and with that ring upon your finger shined and cleaned and your hair smoothed with a bit of oil and this new robe upon you, I swear I could not see a prettier man even in a town."

Now the man heard this and it pleased him and he laughed aloud half sheepishly, and then he remembered himself and said, "And why should I not for once have a new robe for myself? There is nothing ahead but one after another of these young ones, and am I forever to wear my old rags?" And he stooped swiftly and fingered the good stuff in his fingers and while he looked at it the old mother was excited by the thought and she cried, "It is a very fair piece, my son, and if you must have a robe then this is as pretty a blue robe as ever I did see, and I remember once your father had such a robe—was it when we were wed? But no, I was wed in winter, yes, in winter, for I sneezed so at the wedding and the men laughed to see a bride sneezing so—"

But the man asked suddenly and roughly, "How much will it be for a robe?"

Now when the pedlar said the price, at that moment the mother came forth with the money in her hand counted and exact to the last penny and she cried out alarmed, "We can spend no more!"

At that cry of hers some desire hardened in the man and he said wilfully, "But I will have myself a robe cut from this piece and I like it very well so that I will have it for the once! There are those three silver pieces I know we have."

Now those three coins were of good value and coins the mother had brought with her when she came to be wed, and her own mother had handed them to her for her own when she left her home. They were her precious possession and she had never found the hour when she could spend them. Even when she had bought the coffin for the old mother when they thought her dying, she had pinched and borrowed and would not spend her own, and often the thought of those three silver pieces was in her mind for safe riches, and they were there if ever times grew too hard, some war or hardship that might come at any hour and lose them the fruits of their land. With those three coins in the wall she knew they could not starve for a while. So now she cried, "That silver we cannot spend!"

But the man leaped up as swift as a swallow and darted past her in a fury and he went to that cranny and searched in it and seized the silver. Yet the woman was after him, too, and she caught him and held him and hung to him as he ran. But she was not quick enough and never quick enough for his litheness. He threw her aside so that she fell upon the earthen floor, and the child still in her arms, and he ran out shouting as he ran, "Cut me off twelve feet of it and the foot and more to spare that is the custom!"

This the pedlar made haste to do, and he took the silver coins quickly, although indeed they were somewhat less than he had asked, but he was anxious to be away and yet have his stuff sold, too. When the mother came out at last the pedlar was gone and the man stood in the green shade of the tree, the blue stuff bright and new in his two hands, and her silver gone. The old woman sat afraid and when she saw the mother come she began in haste to speak of this or that in a loud creaky voice, "A very pretty blue, my son, and not dear, and a long summer since you had a grass cloth—"

But the man looked blackly at the woman, his face dark and red, and he roared at her, still bold with his anger, "Will you make it, then, or shall I take it to some woman and pay her to make it and tell her my wife will not?"

But the mother said nothing. She sat down again upon her little stool and she sat silent at first, pale and shaken with her fall, and the child she held still screamed in fright. But she paid no heed to him. She set him on the ground to scream, and twisted up afresh the knot of her loosened hair. She panted for a while and swallowed once or twice and at last she said, not looking at the man, "Give it to me then. I will make it."

She was ashamed to have another do it and know the quarrel more than they did now, watching from their doors when they heard the angry cries.

But from that day on the woman harbored this hour against the man. Even while she cut the cloth and shaped it, and she did it well and the best she knew to do, for it was good stuff and worth good care, still she took no pleasure in the work and while she made the robe she stayed hard and silent with the man, and she said no small and easy thing about the day or what had happened in the street or any little thing such as contented women say about a house. And because she was hard with him in these small ways the man was sullen and he did not sing and as soon as he had eaten he went away to the wayside inn and he sat there among the men and drank his tea and gambled far into the night, so that he must needs sleep late the next day. When he did so in usual times she would scold him and keep him miserable until he gave over for peace's sake, but now she let him sleep and she went alone to the fields, hard and silent against him whatever he might do, though her heart was dreary, too, while she kept it hard.

Even when the robe was done at last, and she was long in making it because there was the rice to be set and planted, even when it was done she said nothing of how it looked upon him. She gave it to him and he put it on and he shined his ring with bits of broken stone and he smoothed his hair with oil he poured from the kitchen bottle and he went swaggering down the street.

Yet even when this one and that cried out to him how fine he was and how fine his robe, he took no full sweet pleasure in himself as he might have done. She had said no word to him. No, when he had lingered at the door an instant she went on with her task, bending to the short-handled broom and sweeping about the house and never looking up to ask if the robe fitted him or if his body was suited to its shape, as she was wont to do if she had made him even so much as a pair of new shoes. At last he had even said, half shy, "It seems to me you have sewed this robe better than any robe I ever had, and it fits me as a townsman's does."

But still she would not look up. She set the broom in its corner and went and fetched a roll of cotton wool and set herself to spinning it to thread, since she had used her store in the making of the blue robe. At last she answered bitterly, "At the cost it was to me it should look like an emperor's robe."

But she would not look at him, no, not even when he flung himself down the street. She would not even look at him secretly when his back was turned because she was so bitter against him, although her heart knew the blue robe suited him well.

V

THROUGH that day long the mother watched for the man to come home. It was a day when the fields could be left to their own growing, for the rice was planted in its pools, and in the shallow water and in the warm sunlight the green young plants waved their newly forming heads in the slight winds. There was no need to go out to the land that day.

So the mother sat under the willow tree spinning and the old woman came to sit beside her, glad of one to listen to what she said, and while she talked she unfastened her coat and stretched her thin old withered arms in the hot sun and felt the good heat in her bones, and the children ran naked in the sunshine too. But the mother sat silently on, twisting the spindle with a sure movement between her thumb and the finger she wet on her tongue, and the thread came out close spun and white, and when she had made a length of it she wound it about a bit of bamboo polished smooth to make a spool. She spun as she did all things, firmly and well, and the thread was strong and hard.

Slowly the sun climbed to noon and she put her spinning down and rose.

"He will be coming home soon and hungry for all his blue robe," she said dryly, and the old woman answered, cackling with her ready, feeble laughter, "Oh, aye, what is on a man's belly is not the same as what is in it—"

The mother went then and dipped rice with a gourd from the basket where they kept it stored, and she leveled the gourd with her other hand so not a grain was spilled, and she poured the rice into a basket made of finely split bamboo and went along the path to the pond's edge, and as she went she looked down the street. But she saw no glimpse of new blue. She stepped carefully down the bank and began to wash the rice, dipping the basket into the water and scrubbing the grain with her brown strong hands, dipping it again and again until the rice shone clean and white as wet pearls. On her way back she stooped to pull a head of cabbage where it grew, and threw a handful of grass to the water buffalo tethered under a tree, and so she came again to the house. Now the elder boy came home from the street leading his sister by the hand, and the mother asked him quietly, "Saw you your father on the street or in the inn or at anyone's door?"

"He sat a while at the inn drinking tea this morning," the boy replied, wondering. "And I saw his robe, new and blue, and it was pretty and our cousin when he knew how much it cost said it had cost my father very dear."

66

"Aye, it cost him dear, I swear!" said the mother, suddenly, her voice hard.

And the girl piped up, echoing her brother, "Yes, his robe was blue—even I could see that it was blue."

But the mother said no more. The babe began to weep where he lay sleeping in a winnowing basket and she went and picked him up and opened her coat and held him to her breast, and she suckled him as she went to cook the meal. But first she called to the old woman, "Turn yourself where you sit, old mother, and watch and tell me if you see the new blue of his robe, and I will put the meal on the table."

"I will, then, daughter," called the old dame cheerfully.

Yet when the rice was cooked and flaked, white and dry as the man loved it, still he did not come. When the cabbage was tender and the woman had even made a bit of sweet and sour sauce to pour upon its heart, as he loved it, he did not come.

They waited a while and the old woman grew hungry and faint with the smell of the food in her nostrils and she cried out, in a sudden small anger, being so hungry, "Wait no more for that son of mine! The water is leaking out of my mouth and my belly is as empty as a drum and still he is not here!"

So the mother gave the old woman her bowl then and she fed the children too and even let them eat of the cabbage, only she saved the heart of it for him. She ate also after this, but sparingly for she seemed less zestful in her hunger today, somehow, so there was still much rice left and a good bowlful of the cabbage and this she put carefully away where the wind would catch it and keep it fresh. It would be as good at night as it was now if she heated it again. Then she gave suck to the babe, and he drank his fill and slept, a round, fat, sturdy child, sleeping in the strong sun and brown and red with its heat, and the two children stretched in the shade of the willow tree and slept and the old woman nodded on her bench, and over the whole small hamlet the peace of sleep and the silence of the heat of noonday fell, so that even the beasts stood with drooping, drowsy heads.

Only the mother did not sleep. She took up her spindle and she sat herself in the shade of the willow tree that cast its shadow on the western part of the threshing-floor and she twisted the thread and wound it. But after a while she could not work. Through the morning she had worked steadily and smoothly, twisting and turning and spinning, but now she could not be still. It was as though some strange anxiety gathered like a power in her body. She had never known the man not to come home for his food. She murmured to herself, "It must be he has gone into the town to game or for something or other."

This she had not thought of, but the more she thought upon it the more it seemed true that so he had done. And after a while her cousin-neighbor came out to go to his fields and after a while his wife awoke from where she had sat sleeping by a tree, and she called, "Has your man gone for the day somewhere?"

The mother answered easily, "Aye, he has gone to the town on some business of his own," and the cousin searching slowly among his hoes and spades for what he wanted called in his thin voice, "Aye, I saw him gay in his new blue robe and set for town!"

"Aye," said the woman.

Now her heart eased itself somewhat, and she fell to spinning again with more zeal, since the cousin had seen him set for town. He had gone for a day's pleasure, doubtless, flinging himself off for the day to revenge himself on her. It was what he would do with his new gown and that brass ring of his scrubbed bright and clean and his hair covered with oil. She nursed her anger somewhat at the thought. But her anger was dead, and she could not make it live again, because it was mingled with some strange anxiety still, for all the cousin's words.

The afternoon wore on long and hot. The old woman woke and cried that her mouth was dry as bark and the mother rose and fetched her tea to drink, and the children woke and rolled in the dust a while and rose at last to play, and the babe woke and lay merry in his basket, happy with his sleep.

Still the mother could not rest. If she could have slept she would have, and on any common day she could have dropped easily into sleep even as she worked, since she was so sound and robust that sleep came on her deep and sweet and without her seeking it. But there was some gnawing in her heart today that held her wide awake and as though she listened for some sound that must come.

She rose at last impatient with her waiting and weary of the empty street that was empty for her so long as she did not see the one she sought, and she took up the babe and set him on her thigh and she took her hoe and went to the field, and she called to the old woman, "I go to weed the corn on the south hillside." And as she went she thought to herself that it would be easier if she were not at the house, and the hours would pass more quickly if she pushed her body to some hard labor.

So through the afternoon she worked in the corn field, her face shielded from the sun's heat with a blue cotton kerchief, and up and down she moved her hoe unceasingly among the green young corn. It was but a small, ragged field, for all of their land which could bear it they put into rice, terracing even the hillsides as high as water could be forced, because rice is a more dainty food than corn and sells for higher price.

The sun poured down upon the shadeless hill and beat upon her and soon her coat was wet and dark with her sweat. But she would not rest at all except sometimes to suckle the babe when he cried, and then she sat flat on the earth and suckled him and wiped her hot face and stared across the brilliant summer land, seeing nothing. When he was satisfied she put him down again to work once more and she worked until her body ached and her mind was numb and she thought of nothing now except of those weeds falling under the point of her hoe and withering in the dry hot sunshine. At last the sun rested on the edge of the land and the valley fell into sudden shadow. Then she straightened herself and wiped her wet face with her coat and she muttered aloud, "Surely he will be home waiting—I must go to make his food." And picking up the child from the bed of soft earth where she had laid him she went home.

But he was not there. When she turned the corner of the house he was not there. The old woman was peering anxiously toward the field, and the two children sat upon the doorstep waiting and weary and they cried out when they saw her and she said bewildered, "Your father—is he not come yet?"

"He has not come and we are hungry," cried the boy, and the girl echoed in her broken, childish way, "Not come, and we are hungry!" and sat with her eyes fast shut against the piercing last golden rays of the sun. And the old mother rose and hobbled to the edge of the threshing-floor and called out shrilly to the cousin coming home, "Saw you my son anywhere?"

But the mother cried out in sudden impatience, "Let be, old mother! Do not tell all he is not come!"

"Well, but he does not," said the old woman, peering, troubled.

But the mother said no more. She fetched cold rice for the children and heated a little water and poured it over the rice for the old woman and found a morsel of some old food for the dog, and while they ate she went down the street, the babe upon her arm, to the wayside inn. There were but few guests there now, and only a scattered one or two on his way home to some near village, for it was the hour when men are in their homes and the day's work done. If he were there, she thought, he would be sitting at a table nearest the street where he could hear and see whatever passed, or at a table with a guest, for he would not be alone if he could help it, or if there was a game going on, he would be in the middle of it. But although she stared as she came there was no glint of a new blue robe and no clatter of gambling upon a table. She went and looked within the door then, but he was not there. Only the innkeeper stood resting himself after the evening meal and he leaned against the wall by his stove, his face black with the smoke and grease of many days, for in such a black-ish trade as his it seemed to him but little use to wash himself, seeing he was black again so soon.

"Have you seen the father of my children?" the mother called.

But the innkeeper picked at his teeth with his black fingernail and sucked and called back idly, "He sat here a while in that new blue robe of his this morning and then he went townward for the day." And smelling some new gossip he cried afresh, "What—has aught happened, goodwife?"

"Nothing—nothing—" replied the mother in haste. "He had business in the town and it kept him late, I dare swear, and it may be he will spend the night somewhere and come home tomorrow."

"And what business?" asked the innkeeper suddenly curious.

"How can I know, being but a woman?" she answered and turned away.

But on the way home while her lips called answer back to those who called to her as she passed, she thought of something. When she reached the house she went in and went to that cranny and felt in it. It was empty. Well she knew there had been a precious small store of copper coins there, and a small silver bit, too, because he had sold the rice straw for a good price a day or two ago, being clever at such things, and he brought a good part of the money back. She had taken it from him and counted it and put it into the cranny and there it should be. But it was not there.

Then she knew indeed that he was gone. It came over her in a daze that he was truly gone. She sat down suddenly there in the earthen house upon the earthen floor and holding the babe in her arms she rocked herself back and forth slowly and in silence. Well, he was gone! Here was she with the three children and the old woman, and he gone!

The babe began to fret suddenly and without knowing what she did she opened her bosom to him. The two children came in, the girl whimpering and rubbing her eyes, and the old woman came in leaning on her staff and saying over and over, "I do wonder where is my son. Daughter, did my son say where he was? A very strange thing where my son is gone—"

Then the mother rose and said, "He will be back tomorrow, doubtless, old mother. Lie you down now and sleep. He will be back tomorrow."

The old mother listened and echoed, comforted, "Oh, aye, back tomorrow doubtless," and went to her pallet, feeling through the dim room.

Then the mother led the two children into the dooryard and washed them as her wont was on a summer's night before they slept, and she poured a gourdful of water over each of them, rubbing their smooth brown flesh clean with her palm as she poured. But she did not hear what they said, nor did she heed the girl's moaning of her eyes. Only when they went to the bed and the boy cried, astonished that his father was not come, "And where does my father sleep, then?"—only then did the mother answer out of her daze, "Doubtless in the town, for he will come home tomorrow or in a day or so," and she added in sudden anger, "Doubtless when that bit of money is gone he will be home again," and she added again and most bitterly, "And that new blue robe will be filthy and ready for me to wash already, doubtless!"

And she was somehow glad she could be angry at him, and she held her anger, clinging to it, because it made him seem more near, and she clung to it while she led in the beast and barred the door against the night and she muttered, "I dare swear I shall be just asleep when he comes pounding at the door, even tonight!"

But in the dark night, in the still, hot night, in the silence of the closed room, her anger went out of her and she was afraid. If he did not come back what would she do, a lone woman and young? . . . The bed was enormous, empty. She need take no care tonight, she might spread her arms and legs out as she would. He was gone. Suddenly there fell upon her the hottest longing for that man of hers. These six years she had lain against him. Angry she might be with him in the day, but at night she was near to him again and she forgot his idle ways and his childishness. She remembered now how good and fair he was to look upon, not coarse in the mouth and foul of breath as most men are, but a very fair young man to see, and his teeth as white as rice. So she lay longing for him, and all her anger was gone out of her and only longing left.

When the morning came she rose weary with her sleeplessness, and again she could be hard. When she rose and he did not come and she had turned the beasts out and fed the children and the old woman, she hardened herself and over and over she muttered half aloud, "He will come when his money is gone—very well I know he will come then!"

When the boy stared at the emptiness of the bed and when he asked astonished, "Where is my father still?" she replied sharply and in a sudden loud voice, "I say he is away a day or two, and if any asks you on the street you are to say he is away a day or so."

Nevertheless on that day when the children were off to play here and there she did not go to the fields. No, she set her stool so that she could see through the short single street of the hamlet if any came that way, and while she made answer somehow to the old mother's prattling she thought to herself that the blue robe was so clear a blue she could see it a long way off and she set herself to spinning, and with every twist she gave to the spindle she looked secretly down the road. And she counted over in her mind the money he had taken and how many days it might last, and it seemed to her it could not last more than six or seven days, except he had those nimble lucky fingers of his to game with and so he might make more and stay a little longer, too, before he must come back. Times there were as the morning wore on when she thought she could not bear the old mother's prattling voice any more, but she bore it still for the hope of seeing the man come home perhaps.

When the children wandered home at noon hungry and the boy spied the cabbage bowl set aside for his

father and asked for some, she would not let him have
it. She cuffed him soundly when he asked again and she
answered loudly, "No, it is for your father. If he comes
home tonight he will be hungry and want it all for
himself."

The long still summer's afternoon wore on, and he did
not come, and the sun set in its old way, heavy and full
of golden light, and the valley was filled with the light
for a little while, and the night came and it was deep
and dark and now she refused no more. She set the bowl
before the children and she said, "Eat what you will, for
it will spoil if it is left until another day, and who
knows—" and she dipped up some of the sweet and sour
sauce and gave it to the old woman saying, "Eat it, and
I will make fresh if he comes tomorrow."

"Will he come tomorrow then?" the old woman
asked, and the mother answered sombrely, "Aye, tomorrow perhaps."

That night she laid herself down most sorrowful and
afraid upon her bed and this night she said openly to her
own heart that none knew if he would ever come back
again.

Nevertheless, there was the hope of the seven days
when his money might be gone. One by one the seven
days came, and in each one it seemed to her in the midst
of her waiting as though the day was come for his return. She had never been a woman to gad about the little

hamlet or chatter overmuch with the other women there. But now one after another of these twenty or so came by to see and ask, and they asked where her man was, and they cried, "We are all one house in this hamlet and all somehow related to him and kin," and at last in her pride the mother made a tale of her own and she answered boldly, from a sudden thought in her head, "He has a friend in a far city, and the friend said there was a place there he could work and the wage is good so that we need not wear ourselves upon the land. If the work is not suited to him he will come home soon, but if it be such work as he thinks fit to him, he will not come home until his master gives him holiday."

This she said as calmly as she ever spoke a truth, and the old woman was astounded and she cried, "And why did you not tell me so good a lucky thing, seeing I am his mother?"

And the mother made a further tale and she answered, "He told me not to speak, old mother, because he said your tongue was as loose in your mouth as any pebble and all the street would know more than he did, and if he did not like it he would not have them know it."

"Did he so, then!" cackled the old mother, leaning forward on her staff to peer at her daughter's face, her old empty jaws hanging, and she said half hurt, "It is true I ever was a good talker, daughter, but not so loose as any pebble!"

Again and again the mother told the tale and once

told she added to it now and then to make it seem more perfect in its truth.

Now there was one woman who came often past her house, a widow woman who lived in an elder brother's house, and she had not overmuch to do, being widowed and childless, and she sat all day making little silken flowers upon a shoe she made for herself, and she could ponder long on any little curious thing she heard. So she pondered on this strange thing of a man gone, and one day she thought of something and she ran down the street as fast as she could on her little feet and she cried shrewdly to the mother, "But there has no letter come a long time to this hamlet and I have not heard of any letter coming to that man of yours!"

She went secretly to the only man who knew how to read in the hamlet, and he wrote such few letters as any needed to have written and read such as came for any, and so added a little to his livelihood. This man the widow asked secretly, "Did any letter come for Li The First, who was son to Li The Third in the last generation?"

And when the man said no, the gossip cried out, "But there was a letter, or so his wife says, and but a few days ago."

Then the man grew jealous lest they had taken the letter to some other village writer and he denied again and again, and he said, "Very well I know there was no letter, nor any answering letter, nor has anyone come to me to read or write or to buy a stamp to put on any letter and I am the only one who has such stamps. And there has not come so much as a letter carrier this way for twenty days or more."

Then the widow smelled some strange thing and she told everywhere, whispering that the wife of Li The First lied and there had been no letter and doubtless the husband had run away and left his wife. Had there not been a great quarrel over the new robe, so that the whole hamlet heard them cursing each other, and the man had pushed her down and struck her even? Or so the children said.

But when the talk leaked through to the mother she answered stoutly that what she said was true and that she had made the new blue robe on purpose for the man to go to the far town, and that the quarrel was for another thing. As for the letter, there was no letter but the news had come by word of mouth from a traveling pedlar who had come in from the coast.

Thus did the mother lie steadfastly and well, and the old woman believed the tale heartily and cried out often of her son and how rich he would be, and the mother kept her face calm and smooth and she did not weep as women do when their men run away and shame them. At last the tale seemed true to all, and even the gossip was silenced somewhat and could only mutter darkly over her silken flowers, "We will see—as time comes, we will see if there is money sent or any letter written, or if he comes home ever and again."

So the little stir in the hamlet died down and the minds of people turned to other things and they forgot the mother and her tale.

Then did the mother set herself steadfastly to her life. The seven days were long past and the man did not come and the rice ripened through the days and hung heavy and yellow and ready for the harvest and he did not come. The woman reaped it alone then except for two days when the cousin came and helped her when his own rice was cut and bound in sheaves. She was glad of his help and yet she feared him too, for he was a man of few words, honest and few, and his questions were simple and hard not to answer truthfully. But he worked silently and asked her nothing and he said nothing except the few necessary words he must until he went away, and then he said, "If he is not come when the time is here to divide the grain with the landlord, I will help you then, for the new agent is a wily, clever man, and of a sort ill for a woman to do with alone."

She thanked him quietly, glad of his help, for she knew the agent but a little, since he was new in the last years to those parts, and a townsman who had a false heartiness in all he did and said.

So day had passed into month, and day after day the woman had risen before the dawn and she left the children and the old woman sleeping, and she set their food ready for them to eat when they woke, and taking the babe with her in one arm and in her other hand the short curved sickle she must use in reaping she set out to the fields. The babe was large now and he could sit alone and she set him down upon the earth and let him play as he would, and he filled his hands with earth and put it to his mouth and ate of it and spat it out hating it and yet he forgot and ate of it again until he was covered with the muddy spew. But whatever he did the mother could not heed him. She must work for two and work she did, and if the child cried he must cry until she was weary and could sit down to rest and then she could put her breast to his earthy mouth and let him drink and she was too weary to care for the stains he left upon her.

Handful by handful she reaped the stiff yellow grain, bending to every handful, and she heaped it into sheaves. When gleaners came to her field to glean what she might drop, as beggars and gleaners do at harvest time, she turned on them, her face dark with sweat and earth, and drawn with the bitterness of labor, and she screamed curses at them, and she cried, "Will you glean from a lone woman who has no man to help her? I am poorer than you, you beggars, and you cursed thieves!" And she cursed them so heartily and she so cursed the mothers that bore them and the sons they had themselves that at last they let her fields be, because they were afraid of such powerful cursing.

Then sheaf by sheaf she carried the rice to the threshing-floor and there she threshed it, yoking the buffalo to the rude stone roller they had, and she drove the beast all through the hot still days of autumn, and she drove herself, too. When the grain was threshed, she gathered the empty straw and heaped it and tossed the grain up and winnowed it in the winds that came sometimes.

Now she pressed the boy into labor too and if he lagged or longed to play she cuffed him out of her sheer weariness and the despair of her driven body. But she could not make the ricks. She could not heap the sheaves into the ricks, for this the man had always done, since it was a labor he hated less than some, and he did it always neatly and well and plastered the tops smooth with mud. So she asked the cousin to teach her this one year and she could do it thenceforth with the boy if the man stayed longer than a year, and the cousin came and showed her how and she bent her body to the task and stretched and threw the grass to him as he sat on top of the rick and spread it, and so the rice was harvested.

She was bone-thin now with her labor and with being too often weary, and every ounce of flesh was gone from her, and her skin was burnt a dark brown except the red of cheeks and lips. Only the milk stayed in her breasts rich and full. Some women there are whose food

83

goes all to their own fat and none to child or food for child, but this woman was made for children, and her motherhood would rob her own body ruthlessly if there was any need for child.

Then came the day set for measuring out the landlord's share of all the harvest. Now this landlord of the hamlet and the fields about it never came himself to fetch his share. He lived an idle rich man in some far city or other, since the land was his from his fathers, and he sent in his place his agent, and this year it was a new agent, for his old agent had left him the last year, being rich enough after twenty years to cease his labors. This new agent came now and he came to every farmer in that hamlet, and the mother waited at her own door, the grain heaped on the threshing-floor and waiting, and the agent came.

He was a townsman, head to foot, a tall, smooth man, his gown gray silk and leathern shoes on his feet, and he had a large smooth hand he put often to his shaven lip, and when he moved a scent of some sort came from him. The mother hung back when he came and when he called, "Where is the farmer?" the woman waited and let the old mother pipe forth, "My son he works in the city now, and there be only we upon the land."

And the woman sent the lad for the cousin and she waited silently, coming forward to hand the man his tea but saying nothing but common greeting, yet feeling his eyes somehow hot upon her bare feet and on her face.

THE MOTHER

And she stood by while the cousin measured off the grain for her, and measured the share the agent took for his own, and the woman was glad she needed to say nothing nor even come near to see the weight, so honest was her cousin. But she saw the grain divided and hard it was too, as it was hard for every farmer, to give to this smooth townsman his own share in what they had labored on. But they gave grimly, and so did she, knowing that if they did not they would suffer, and besides the landlord's share they gave the agent a fat fowl or two or a measure of rice or some eggs or even silver for his private fee.

More than this, when all the grain was measured out the village must set a feast before the agent and every house must give a dish. Even in this lonely year the mother caught a fowl and killed it and cooked it for the feast, steaming it gently and long until it was done and while the shape was whole and the skin unbroken, yet was the flesh so tender that when the first chopsticks touched it it would fall apart. The savor of that fowl and its smell when it had cooked so many hours were more than the children could endure and they hung about the kitchen and the boy cried, "I wish it were for us—I wish we ever could eat a fowl ourselves!"

But the mother was bitter with her weariness and she answered, "Who can eat such meat except a rich man?"

Nevertheless when the feast was over she went to the littered table where the men had sat and she picked up

85

a bone left from her fowl and a little skin was hanging to it and a shred of meat and she took it and gave it to the lad to suck and she said, "Hasten and grow big, my son, and you can eat at table with them too."

Then the boy asked innocently, "Do you think my father will let me?"

The mother answered bitterly, "If he is not here you shall eat in his place, that I swear."

Thus the year wore on to late autumn. Almost the children had forgotten that there had ever been another in the bed except themselves and their mother, and even the old woman seldom thought to ask of her son, because the chill winds set her old bones aching, and she had enough to do to search for this warm spot and that out of wind and in the sun, and she complained incessantly because the winds shifted so, and because every year the sun seemed cooler than the year before.

The boy worked daily now in small ways and took it as his duty. Every day when there was no other task he led the buffalo to the hill lands and let it feed on the short grass, lying upon its back the whole day through, or coming down to leap upon some grave and sit there catching crickets in the grass and weaving little cages for them out of stems of grass. When he came home at night he hung the cages by the door, and the crickets chirped and the sound pleased the babe and his sister.

But soon the wild grass on the hills browned with

coming winter and the summer flowers among the grass bore seed and the byways were gay with purple asters and with small yellow wild chrysanthemums, which are the flowers of autumn, and it was time to cut the grass for winter's fuel. Then the boy went with his mother and all day she cut the dried grass with her short-handled sickle and the boy twisted rope of grass and bound what she cut into sheaves. Everywhere over all the mountain sides there were spots of blue and these were people like themselves cutting and binding the brown grass into sheaves. In the evening when the sun set and the night air came down chill from the hill tops the people all went winding homeward through the narrow hilly paths, each loaded with two great sheaves upon a pole across the shoulder, and so did the mother also, and the boy with two little sheaves.

When they came home the first thing the mother did was to seize the babe and ease her breasts of their load of milk and the child drank hungrily, having had but rice gruel in the day. The old woman these cold early nights crept into bed to warm herself as soon as the sun was set and the little girl came feeling her way out into the last light of day, wincing a little even in that pale light, and she sat smiling on the threshold, rejoicing in her brother's coming, for she missed him now he had to work.

So did the autumn pass, and here was the ground to be ploughed for wheat and the wheat sown and the mother taught the lad how to scatter it so that a passing wind would help him and how to watch the wind, too, and not let the grain fall too thickly here and too scanty there. Then the winter came when the wheat was sprouted but a little, and the fields shrank and hardened in the oncoming cold. Now the mother drew the winter garments out from under her bed where she kept them and she sunned them and made them ready to wear. But the rough work of the summer and the autumn had so torn her hands that even the coarse cotton cloth caught at the cracks upon them and her fingers were stiff and hard, although shapely still in the bone.

Yet she worked on, sitting now in the doorway to be in the southern sun and out of the sharp wind and first she tended to the old woman's garments, since she felt the chill so much. And she bade the old woman stay in bed a day or two and take off the red shroud she wore, and in between the stuff and its lining she put back the cotton wadding she had taken out when summer came, and the old woman lay snug and chattered happily and cried, "Shall I outlast this shroud, do you think, daughter-in-law? In summer time I feel I shall, but when the winter comes I am not sure, because my food does not heat me as once it did."

And the mother answered absently, "Oh, you will last, I dare swear, old mother, and I never saw such an old crone for lasting on when others have gone the common way."

88

Then the old woman cackled full of pleasure and she cackled, laughing and coughing, "Aye, a very lasting sort I be, I know!" and lay content and waited for her shroud to be made warm for her again.

And the mother mended the children's clothing, but the girl's garments she must give to the babe, and the boy's to the girl, so had they all three grown in the year. Then came the question of what the lad would wear to keep him warm. There was the man's padded coat and there the trousers that he had worn those three winters gone and he had torn them and she had mended them at wrist and neck, and in the front was a long tear where the buffalo's horn had caught one day when he was angry at the beast and had jerked the rope passed through its nostrils, so that it tossed its head in agony.

But she could not bear to cut them small to the lad's shape. She turned the garments over pondering and aching and at last she muttered, "What if he should come— I will not do it yet."

But there the boy was not clad for winter and he waited shivering in the chill of morning and evening, and at last she set her lips and made the garments small for him and she comforted herself and said in her heart, "If he comes we can sell some of the rice and buy new ones. If he should come at the new year he will take pleasure in the new garments."

So the winter wore on and it seemed to the woman that the man must surely come at the new year, a time when all men go to their homes if they still live and are not beggars. So when any asked her she began to say, "He will come home for the new year festival," and the old mother said a score of times a day, "When my son comes at new year . . ." and the children hoped too for the day. Now and again the gossip would smile and say in her malice, and she was making herself a fine new pair of shoes against the day of festival, "It is strange no letter comes from that man of yours, and I know none comes, for the letter writer tells me so."

Then the mother would answer with outward calm, "But I have heard several times by mouth of one who passed, and my man and I have never held with much writing and the good money that must go out for it, and no knowing, either, what hired writers forget to say and it is all written and it is public for the whole street to know when once it does come to me. I am glad he sends no letters."

So did she silence the gossip, and so much she said he would come at the new year that truly it seemed to her he would. The time drew near and everyone in the hamlet was busy for the feast, and she must needs be busy, too, not only for the children, to make them new shoes and wash their garments clean and make a new cap for the babe, but she must be busy for the man, also. She filled two great baskets with the rice, all she dared to spare, and carried them to the town, and sold them at but a little less in price than the man did, and this was well enough, seeing she was a woman bargaining alone with men. With the money she bought two red candles and incense to burn before the god and red letters of luck to paste upon the tools and on the plough and farm things that she used, and she bought a little lard and sugar to make sweet cakes for the day. Then with what was left she went into a cloth shop and bought twenty feet or so of good blue cotton cloth and to another shop and bought five pounds of carded cotton wool for padding.

Yes, she was so sure by now he would come that she even set her scissors in that cloth and she cut it slowly and with pains and care and she made a coat and trousers of the good stuff and padded them evenly and quilted them, and so she finished the garments to the last button she made of bits of cloth twisted hard and sewed fast. Then she put the garments away against his coming, and to all of them it seemed the garments brought the man more nearly home again.

But the day dawned and he did not come. No, all day long they sat in their clean clothes, the children clean and frightened lest they soil themselves, and the old woman careful not to spill her food upon her lap, and the mother made herself to smile steadfastly all through the day, and she told them all, "It is still day yet, and he may yet come in the day." There came those to the door who had been good fellows with her man and they came to wish him well if he were come, and she pressed tea on them and the little cakes and when they asked she said, "Truly he may come today, but it may be his master cannot spare him days enough to come so far, and I hear his master loves him well and leans on him."

And when the next day the women came she said this also and she smiled and seemed at ease and said, "Since he is not come, there will come word soon, I swear, and tell me why," and then she spoke of other things.

So the days passed and she talked easily and the children and the old woman believed what she said, trusting her in everything.

But in the nights, in the dark nights, she wept silently and most bitterly. Partly she wept because he was gone, but sometimes she wept, too, because she was so put to shame, and sometimes she wept because she was a lone woman and life seemed too hard for her with these four leaning on her.

One day when she sat thinking of her weeping it came to her that at least she could spare herself the shame. Yes, when she thought of the money she had spent for his new garments and he did not come, and of the cakes she had made and of the incense burned to pray for him, and he did not come, and when she thought of the gossip's sly looks and all her whispered hints and the wondering doubtful looks of even her good cousin, when time passed and still the man did not come, then it seemed to her she must spare herself the shame.

And she wiped her tears away and plotted and she thought of this to do. She carried all the rice she could spare into the city and the straw she had to spare and she sold it. When she had the silver in her hand she asked for a paper bit that is as good as silver, and with it she went to a letter writer, a strange man in that town she did not know, and he sat in his little booth beside the Confucian temple. She sat down on the little bench near by, and she said, "I have a letter to write for a brother who is working and is not free to go home, and so say what I tell you. He is ill upon his bed, and I write for him."

Then the old man took out his spectacles and stopped staring at the passersby, and he took a sheet of new paper and he wet his brush upon the block of ink and looked at her and said, "Say on, then, but tell me first the brother's wife's name and where her home is and what your name is too."

Then the mother told him, "It is my brother-in-law who bids me write the letter to his wife and he lives in a city from whence I am but come newly, and my name is no matter," and she gave her husband's name for brother and the name of a far city she had known once to be near her girlhood home, and then for her brother's wife's name she gave her own name and where her hamlet was and she said, "Here is what he has to tell his wife. Tell her, 'I am working hard and I have a good place and I have what I like to eat and a kind master, and all I need to do is to fetch his pipe and tea and take his messages to his friends. I have my food and three silver pieces a month besides, and out of my wage I have saved ten pieces that I have changed to a paper bit as good these days as silver. Use them for my mother and yourself and the children.' "

Then she sat and waited and the old man wrote slowly and for a long time and at last he said, "Is that all?"

And she said, "No, I have this more to say. Say, 'I could not come at the new year because my master loves me so he could not spare me, but if I can I will come another year, and if I cannot even so I will send you my wage as I am able once a year, as much as I can spare.' "

And again the old man wrote and she said when she had thought a while, "One more thing there is he is to say. Say, 'Tell my old mother I shall bring red stuff for her third shroud when I come, as good stout stuff as can be bought.' "

So the letter was complete and the old man signed the letter and sealed it and set the superscription and he spat upon a stamp and put it on, and said that he would post it in the place he knew. And she paid his fee and went home, and this was the thing she had plotted when she wiped her tears away.

VI

SOME seven days after that day a letter carrier who carried letters in a bag upon his shoulder passed by, a new thing in these later days, for in old days there were no such men, and to the folk of this hamlet it was ever a magic miracle that letters could be come by like this, but so they were, nevertheless. And now this man took a letter from his bag and held it and he stared at the mother and he said, "Are you the wife of one surnamed Li?"

Then she knew her letter had come and she said, "I am that one," and he said, "Then this is yours and it is from your man, wherever he is, for his name is written there." So he gave her the letter.

Then she made herself cry out and she summoned false joy somehow and she cried to the old woman, "Here is a letter from your son!" And to the children she said, "Here is your father's letter come!" They could scarcely wait until it was read, and the woman washed herself and put on a clean coat and combed her hair smoothly, and while she did she heard the old mother call out to the cousin's wife, "My son's letter is come!" and when she had said it she laughed and fell to coughing and laughing until the cousin's wife across the way grew frightened at such a turmoil in the weak old body and ran over and rubbed her back and cried in her hearty kind way, "Good mother, do not let it kill you, I pray!" And when the mother came out clean and smiling she said in her same way, "Here be this old crone choking herself because a letter is come!" and the mother made her smile shine out and she said, "So it has and here it is," and held the letter out for the other one to see.

When she went down the street they all came crowding with her as she went, for the lad followed grinning and saying to all who asked that his father's letter was come, and the little girl came after him, clinging to his coat, and since it was winter still and little to be done, the idle men and women followed, too, and they all crowded to the letter writer's house, who was astonished at such a houseful coming in so suddenly. But when he heard what the matter was he took the letter and studied it a while and he turned it this way and that and stared at it, and at last he said gravely and as the first thing to be said, "It is from your husband."

"That I guessed," the mother said, and the gossip who was in the crowd called out, "And what other man would it be, good man?" And all the crowd roared with ready laughter.

Then the letter writer began to read the letter to her slowly and silence fell and the mother listened and the children and all the crowd, and at every word he paused to explain its full meaning, partly because it is true written and spoken words are not the same, but partly, too, to show how learned he was. And the mother listened as though she had never heard one word of it before, and she nodded at every word, and when he came to that place where it said there was money sent, the man raised his voice very loud and clear at such a serious thing, and those in the crowd gaped and cried out, "But was there money in it?" Then the woman nodded and she opened her hand and showed the paper piece into which she had changed her own silver, and she gave it to the letter writer to see, and he said hushed and solemnly, "It is true I see a ten, and it must be it is worth ten pieces of silver."

Then all the crowd must see it and there was a picture of a fat whiskered general on the paper and when the gossip saw it she cried out aghast, "Why, goodwife, how your man is changed!" for she supposed it was a picture of the man himself, and none of them was sure it was not except the woman and she said, "It is not my man, I know." And the letter writer guessed and said, "Doubtless it is his master." And so they all looked at it again and cried how rich and fed he looked. Thus all the crowd were silent with wonder and with envy, and they watched while the mother folded the bit of precious paper into her hand and held it there closely.

So was the letter read and when the old man had finished it and folded it into its case again, he said gravely, "You are a very lucky wife and it is not every countrywoman whose man could go into a great city and find so good a place, or who if he did would send back his wage like that either, and so many places as I hear there are in towns to spend money in."

Then all the crowd fell back in respect for her, and she walked proudly home, the children following her and sharing in their mother's glory, and when the mother was come she told it all to the old mother and especially did the old soul laugh with pleasure to hear what her son said of the third shroud and she cried out in her trembling, cracking voice and struck her skinny knees with pleasure, "That son of mine! I do swear there was never one like him! And doubtless that town stuff is very fine good stuff." Then she grew a trifle grave and she said wistfully, "Aye, daughter, if it be as good as he says, I doubt I can wear it out before I die. It may be that one will be my last shroud."

The lad looked grave, too, when he saw his grandmother look so, and he cried loyally, "No, grandmother, it will not, for you have lasted two, and this one cannot be as strong as two!"

Then the old soul was cheered again and laughed to hear the boy so clever, and she said to the mother, "Very well you remembered all he said, daughter, and almost as if you read the words yourself."

"Aye," said the mother quietly, "I remembered every word." And she went alone into the house and stood

behind the door and wept silently, and the letter and
even the bit of paper that was the same as silver were but
ashes for all her pride. They were worthless for her when
she was alone; there was no meaning in them then.

Nevertheless, the mother's plot worked well enough
and hereafter in the hamlet there was none who mocked
at her or hinted she was a woman whose man had left
her. Rather did she need to harden her heart toward
them now, because since it was known she had the paper
money and that there would come more next year like
it, some came to borrow of her secretly, the old letter
writer one, and besides him an idle man or two who
sent his wife to ask for him, and the woman was hard
put to it to refuse since all in the hamlet were some sort
of kin and all surnamed Li, but she said this and that,
and that she owed the money for a debt and that she
had spent it already or some such thing. And some cried
out at her when they talked together idly in a dooryard,
and the gossip said before her meaningfully how much a
bit of cloth cost these days and even a needle or two
was costly and a few strands of silken thread to make a
flower on a shoe for color, and they all took care to cry
if she were there, "Well is it for such as you, and a very
lucky destiny, that you have no need to think thrice over
a penny, while your man is out earning silver and send-
ing it to you and you have it over and above what is
wrest from the bitter land!" And sometimes a man
would call, "I doubt it is a good thing to have so rich a

woman in our hamlet lest the robbers come. Aye, robbers come where riches are, as flies to any honey!"

It seemed to her at last that daily this bit of paper grew more troublesome, not only because of what the gossip said, and because this one and that one among the men would ask to see it close, but because she too was not used to money being of paper and she grew to hate the thing because she was ever afraid the wind might blow it away or the rats gnaw it or the children find it and think it nothing and tear it in play, and every day she must look to see if it were safe in the basket of stored rice where she kept it hid, because she was afraid it would mold in the earthen wall and rot away there. At last the thing grew such a burden on her that one day when she saw the cousin start for the town she ran to him and whispered, "Change me this bit of paper into hard silver, I pray, so that I can feel it in my hand, because this bit of paper seems nothing when I hold it."

So the cousin took it and being a righteous honest man he changed it into silver, good and sound in every piece, and when he was back at her door again he struck each piece upon another to show how sound all were. The mother was grateful to him and she said, although half unwillingly too, except she did not wish to be thought small in mind, "Take a piece of it for your trouble, cousin, and for your help in harvest, for well I know you need it and your wife swelling with another child."

But though he stared hard at the silver and sucked

his breath in without knowing he did and blinked his eyes once or twice with longing he would not take it and he said quickly before his longing grew too much for him, because indeed he was a good and honest man, "No, cousin's wife, for you are a lone woman and I am able to work yet."

"Well, if you need to borrow then," she said and quickly took the silver out of sight, for well she knew no man can look at silver long, however good he is, and not grow weak with longing.

In that night while the children and the old woman slept the mother rose and lit the candle and dug a hole with her hoe into the hard earth of the floor and there she hid the ten pieces of silver, but first she wrapped them in a bit of rag to keep the earth from them. The buffalo turned and stared with its great dull eyes, and the fowls woke under the bed and looked out at her with this eye and then with that and clucked faintly, astonished at this strange thing in the night. But the woman filled the hole and walked a while on it to make it beaten smooth and like the rest. Then she laid herself down again in the darkness.

It was the strangest thing, but as she lay there awake and yet half dreaming, almost she forgot it was her own silver she had buried and silver she gained from the harvest she had cut herself, bending her back in weariness to every handful of the grain. Yes, she forgot this, and it seemed to her almost that the man had truly sent it to her, and that it was a something over and beyond her own, and she murmured to her heart, "It is in place of the silver bits he took and spent for that blue gown, and better, for it is more," and she forgave him for that thing he had done, and so she fell into sleep.

Thereafter when one asked to see the paper bit she answered tranquilly, "I have changed it for common silver and spent it," and when the gossip heard it she cried out, her loose mouth ajar, "But have you spent it all?" the mother answered easily and she smiled, "Aye, I have spent it all for this and that, and a new pot or two and cloth and this and that, and why not when there is more to come?" And she went in the house and fetched out the new garments she had made for the man to wear if he came home and she said, "Here is some of the cloth such as I bought with it," and they all stared at it and pinched the stuff and cried out that it was a very good strong cloth and the gossip said unwillingly, "You are a very good woman, I can swear, to spend the money, even to a share, upon clothes for him, and not all for yourself, or for the children."

Then the mother answered steadfastly, "But we are well content with each other, my man and I, and I did spend some upon myself, for I gave some to a silversmith and bade him fashion me some earrings and a ring for my hand, for my man did ever say he wanted me to have them when we had something over and to spare."

The old woman had listened to this all and now she

cried out, "I swear my son is just such a man as she says, and he is to buy me my third shroud and of the best town stuff. A very good son, neighbors, and I wish as good a one to each of you, and especially to you, cousin's wife, for I see your belly swollen as a ripe melon!"

Then the goodwives laughed and went away again, one by one, for it was evening time. But when they were gone the mother groaned within herself at such a great tale as she had told, and she reproached herself and said in her own heart, "Now why need I have told such a vast tale, and could not be content with what was told already? Where shall I find money for those trinkets? Yet must I somehow do it to save myself the truth."

And she sighed to think of all the burden she had put upon herself.

VII

ONCE more the spring came on, and now the mother must set herself hard to the land and she pressed the boy into the labor, too, and she taught him how to drive the beast. Push the plough he could not, being so light and small, but he could run behind the beast and beat its thick slaty hide, and because its hide was so thick that all his strength could not pierce it, she fastened a sharp peg into a bamboo length and bade the boy beat with that to stir the beast out of its vast indolence.

The girl child, too, the mother pressed into small simple tasks, for the old woman grew more idle as she grew older, and forgetful so that all she remembered was to know if she were hungry or athirst. Only did she stir if the younger boy cried and wanted something in his lusty way, for the grandmother loved this youngest one. So the mother taught the girl to wash the noon's rice at the pond, but she let her do it first before she set forth to the fields, lest the child with her half-seeing eyes fall into the pool and drown, and she taught her how to cook the rice, too, against their coming, though she was so small she scarce could reach the cauldron lid. She taught this little thing even to light the fire and keep it blazing, and this the little girl did very well, too, and she was patient when the smoke came out and flew into her eyes and smarted on the lids, and she did not complain at anything, for she understood that now the house was without the father, and the mother must do for them all. Nevertheless when the task was done she went into the house where it was dark even at noonday and there she sat and wiped her streaming eyes with a bit of old cloth she kept for this and she bore the pain as best she could.

The babe could walk, too, now that spring was come, for in the winter he had not tried, being burdened with his padded clothes so heavily that even though he fell he could not rise until someone passed by his way and set him right again. Now he ate what he would and thrived. But the mother let him suckle still because it gave her some vague comfort, although her breasts were well-nigh dry by now. Still it was a comfort to her in some dumb sweet way that the child clung to her breast and that he ran to meet her when he saw her coming home at night and cried to drink what little was there for him.

Thus the early spring came into full mild spring, and the mother labored hard with the boy beside her all day long, and the fields were ploughed somehow, if not so straight or deep as the man had ploughed them, for it had been what he had always done in springs past, while she sowed the seed. But beans were put in and young cabbage and the radishes to be sold at market, and soon the rape budded again and sent up its early heads and bloomed yellow and gold. So did she labor that well-nigh she forgot the man, she was so weary every night, and so dead in sleep she scarcely could rise again at dawn.

But there came a day when she remembered him.

Now the hour was come when the cousin's wife was due to give birth and she sent a child to go and call the mother, who was her friend and nearest neighbor, and the child came to the field where the mother was working, the sweet spring wind blowing her loose coat as she worked and cooling her sweat as soon as it came.

The child was a young girl, and she called out, "Good aunt, my mother's hour is come, and she says will you hasten, for you know how quick she is, and she sits ready and waiting for you to catch the babe!"

The mother straightened her bent back then and answered, "Aye, tell her I will come," and she turned to the lad and said, "Take my hoe and weed these beans as best you can while I am gone. It will not be above an hour or so, if she is as quick as she always is."

So saying she went across the fields and followed behind the girl who ran ahead, and as the woman walked it came over her in some new way how sweet a day this was. Living in this valley every day and laboring as she must, she never thought to lift her head to see what the world was about her, but her whole thought was on the

THE MOTHER

land or in her house and her eyes bent to them always. But now she lifted her head as she walked and saw. The willows were full of tender leaves shining green, and the white blossoms of the pear trees were full blown this day and drifting in the winds, and here and there a pomegranate tree flamed scarlet in its early leaves. The wind, too, was very warm, and it came in sudden gusts and died again, and she did not know which was sweeter, the deep warm silence when the wind died and the smell of the earth came up from the ploughed fields, or the windy fragrance of the gusts. But walking thus in the silences and in the sudden winds, she felt her body strong and full and young, and a great new longing seized her for the man.

Nearly every spring she had given birth, nearly every spring since she was wed, but this spring was her body barren. Once it had seemed a usual common thing to bear a child, and a thing to be done again and again, but now it seemed a joy she had not seen was joy until now, and her loneliness came over her like a pain and her breasts ached when she thought of the thing, and it was this, that she would never bear a child again in such a spring unless her man came home. Suddenly her longing streamed out of her like a cry, "Oh—come home— come home!"

Yes, she seemed to hear her own voice cry the words, and she stopped, frightened lest she had called them out before the young girl. Yet she had not cried aloud, and

when she stopped there was but the voice of the wind
and the loud bright music of a blackbird in a pomegranate tree.

And when she went into the dark room and saw the
round plain face of her cousin's wife drawn out of its
roundness and dark with sweat and the usual laughter
gone from it and the gravity of pain set there instead,
the mother's own body felt full and heavy as though it
were she who bore the child and not this other one. And
when the child came and she caught him and wrapped
him in a bit of cloth and when she was free to go back
to the field, she could not go. No, she went back to her
own house listlessly, and when the old woman cried,
"What—is it time for food? But I do not feel my hunger
yet!" and when the girl came running out of the house
shading her eyes with her hand, and crying, "Is it time
already to light the fire, mother?" the mother answered
listlessly, "No, it is too early, but I am strangely weary
today and I will rest a while," and she went and laid
herself upon the bed.

But she could not rest, and soon she rose and took
up the little boy and held him fiercely and she laid her
bosom open and would have had him suckle. But the
child was astonished at her fierceness, being unused to it,
and he was not hungry yet and he was full of play, and
so he struggled and straightened himself and pushed her
breast away and would not have it. Then the mother felt
a strange sullen anger rise in her and she cuffed him and

set him hard upon the ground and he screamed and she muttered, "Ever you will suck when I will not, and now when I will then you are not hungry!"

And she was pleased in the strangest way, half bitterly, because he lay and wept. But the old woman cried out to hear his roaring and the little girl ran to pick him up. Then the mother felt her softness come back in her and she would not let the girl have him, but she lifted him suddenly herself and smoothed the dust from him, and wiped his tearful face with her palm, and she blamed herself secretly with a sort of shame that she had made the child suffer for her own pain.

But the child never loved her breast so well again from that hour, and so even that small comfort she had had was taken from her.

VIII

NOW from her youth up this woman had been
ever a creature of deep still heats. She was not
as some women are, quick to look at this young
man and that and appraising any man who passed. No,
she was a woman of a very deep heart, shy to the depths
of it, and until she was properly wed even when she was
alone her thoughts had not turned to men for their own
sake, and if strange longings rose from within her deeply
she never looked at them to see what they were or why
they came, but she went on steadfastly to some task she
had to do, and bore her longing patiently and in a waiting silence. Only when she was wed and had known a
man for all he was did some clearness come to her, some
distillation of that deep dumb longing, so that even
while she scolded her man sometimes and was angry
with him, she knew she could not live without him.
That thick, impatient longing in her could even heap
itself like thunderous clouds into a causeless anger against
the man she loved until it resolved itself and they clung
each to each, and she was satisfied in the old and simple
way and so was made tranquil again.

Yet the man was never enough. In himself he was

never enough. She must conceive by him and feel a child take life and shape within her. Then was the act complete and while the child moved and grew she went in a daze of happiness, being fulfilled. Yes, even when she bawled her little angers at her children when they were under her feet and when they cried and whimpered for this and that and were wilful as children must be, yet she never saw the signs of new birth upon herself without a sweet content of body, as though she were fed and rested and had slept so that her body wanted nothing more.

So had she ever loved a babe. Even so it had been in the old days when she was a girl in her father's house and in a village but a little larger than this hamlet set in hills. Her father's house was full of little children and she was the eldest and like a mother to them; yet even when she was weary with the day's toil and the children running under her feet were a trial to her so that she shouted at them to be out of her way, yet never even when she shouted was she really out of love with them. There was always something in their smallness that weakened her heart, and many a time she would pick up a little child, whether of their own house or of some neighbor's, and hold him against her and smell of him hard and fondle him as long as he would bear it, because it was some passionate pleasure to her to feel a little child, although she did not know why.

So everything young and leaning on her drew her

heart out. In the spring she loved the young chicks and ducklings coming from the shell, and when a mother hen forsook her nest for some cause and left the eggs half hatched she it was who took the eggs and made a bag and slipped them against her warm flesh and walked lightly and carefully until the young chicks hatched. She it was who was most faithful to feed the small silk-worms, and took pleasure in their growing and she watched them from the time when they were scarcely more than bits of living thread until they grew great and fat, and when they burst their cocoons and came forth moths and mated, moth to moth, she felt that seeking and that satisfaction in her own body.

Once when the children of her father's house were grown out of babyhood and she was nearly ready to be wed herself there was a certain thing that happened to her, and it roused her as no man had ever done yet. There was one little boy who was too young to walk, a neighbor's child, a round fat boy whose elder sister carried him about that whole summer long, naked and caught in a strip of cloth upon her back. And sometimes the mother, young then and waiting to be wed, would untie this strip and take the child from the little girl's back, and the little girl would dart off to her play, glad to be released from her burden for a while.

It came to be so then that every day the young girl, the mother, grew to look for this little moon-faced boy and out of all the other children of the village he was the greatest joy to her, her favorite, and she held him and smelled of his fat palms and took pleasure in his round cheeks and in his little rosy mouth, and she carried him about with her, setting him astride her sturdy hip, and when her own mother cried, "What—had you not enough of children in this house so that when I am through my bearing you must go and seek another's child?" she answered laughing, "I am never weary of babes, I think!"

Soon without her knowing it this child came to rouse in her a longing she had never known before. Sons she wanted as all women did, and she had always taken it as her right that she would have sons one day. But this robust and calm-eyed child roused more than wish of sons in her, and what had first been play with the child became something more, some deep and secret passion for what she did not know.

She made excuse then when the child was in her arms to get away with him alone and all the others were busy here or there in field or kitchen, and the child's sister was glad to be away, and the young girl sat and held the fair sound child strained against herself. She murmured to him and nursed him in her arms and felt this little, fat, round body helpless against her. Sometimes, since he was still nearly toothless, she chewed up rice or a cake for him and thrust the food into his little lips from hers, and when he sucked it solemnly, surprised at what he felt in his mouth suddenly, she laughed, but she did not know why she laughed, for she was not merry, seeing there was such a fierce, deep, painful longing in her which she did not know how to ease.

One day soon before her marriage day she had the child thus alone and it grew late toward noon and the little girl did not come as early as usual to take the child to his mother to be fed, and the child fretted and tossed himself and would not be still. Then the young girl, seeing his hunger, and driven by some dim fierce passion she did not understand but only felt in her blood urging her on, went into her room and shut the door fast and with trembling hands she undid her coat and put the child to her own young slender breast and he laid hold on it lustily and sucked hard at it. Then she, standing there staring into his baby face, felt such a tumult in her blood as she had never dreamed of and the tears came into her eyes and sounds rose to her lips, broken sounds that were not words, and she held him strained against her and did not know what it was she felt within herself, full and yearning and passionate, greater than the child she held, greater than herself.

Then the moment broke. Her little breast was empty and the child wailed in disappointment and she fastened her coat again and was ashamed somehow of what she had done and she went quickly out and the little girl his sister came running in and seized him and ran with him to his own mother.

But to the young girl the moment was an awakening

THE MOTHER

and more almost than marriage. Ever after even the man
she wed was most to her because he was a part of motherhood, and not for his own sake only did she love him.

So had it been with her in her raw youth. Now with
her body ripe and knowing all and herself in all her
prime of womanhood she was left, woman alone, and
every day the children grew up taller and every day
they grew further from their babyhood they seemed less
her own.

The elder boy shot up tall and thin and silent, and
he said little but strained himself at heavy tasks. When
the mother would have taken up the rude wooden plough
to carry it back to the house at the end of the day, he
seized it and held it like a yoke across his own thin
shoulders and staggered with it over the clodded earth,
and she was so weary oftentimes she let him do it. He
it was now who pulled the pails of water from the well
and fed the buffalo, and he struggled his whole share
and more in the field, as though he were his own
father.

Yet in all this he strained away from the woman, his
mother, in some secret way, sharing with her in the
labor most dutifully, and yet often wilful too, and it
seemed to her he was parted from her flesh in some way
she could not understand, not liking to be near her and
standing off as though there were some smell about her
that he could not bear. Oftentimes they quarreled over

THE MOTHER

a slight cause, such as if she bade him hold his hoe better and he would not but would hold it in his own way, even though it was harder to wield when he held it so. Over such a small thing they quarreled and over many other like small things. Yet each knew dimly that this was not the true cause of quarrel either, but some deeper thing which neither could perceive.

The girl, too, was never any cause of joy to her, with her poor eyes half blind. Still the child did her patient best and she complained no more now as she once did, and now that the younger boy could walk and run and loved best to be in the street brawling and playing with others like him, the girl would come sometimes to the field where the mother and the lad worked. But even there she was more care than help, especially if it were in some field of small weak seedlings, for she was so blind that when she would have pulled the weeds she did not see them well and many a time she pulled a seedling, thinking it a weed, so that the boy called out in anger, "Go home, you girl, for I do swear you are no use to us here. Go and sit beside the old grandmother!"

And when she rose at this, half smiling but deeply hurt too, he cried at her again shrilly, "Now see where you tread, you clumsy thing, for you are walking on the seedlings now!"

So she made haste to get out of the field then, too proud to stay, and the mother was torn between these two, her son and the poor half blind girl, and she felt

117

the hearts of both, the lad's heart weary with labor too bitter for his age, and the girl's too patient with her pain, and she said sighing, as the girl went away, "It is true, poor thing, you are very little use, nor even can you sew with those eyes as they are. But go you home and sweep the floor and set the food ready and light the fire. Such things you do well enough. Watch the little one and see he does not fall in the pond, for he is the boldest, wilfulest of you all, and pour a little tea sometimes for the old one. There your duty is and you are help to me there. And when I have a little time I will go and seek a balm of some kind for your eyes."

So she comforted the girl, but the girl was little comfort to her, sitting silent hour after hour and wiping her wet aching lids, and smiling in her fixed and patient way. And looking at her sometimes and hearing her lad's angers and seeing the younger one's eagerness to be away at play, the mother wondered bitterly how it could be that when they were babes they were so fair and pleasant to her, and now no comfort.

Yes, oftentimes in the evening this mother looked across the way to her cousin's house and envied it most sorely. There was the good and honest husband, a plain and earth-soiled man, not clean and pretty as her man had been, but still well enough and going to his daily work and coming home to be fed and to sleep as men should, and there were his children he begot regularly and well, and there the mother sat, easy and merry and well content with her last babe upon her knees, a shallow merry soul and her mouth always open and her tongue clacking, but kindly and a good neighbor. Often she ran to share some bit of meat with the mother, or gave the children a handful of fruit, or a little paper flower she made for the girl to thrust into her hair. It was a good, full, contented house, and the mother envied it, and in her the longing grew, deep and sullen and unsatisfied.

IX

IF she could have forgotten the man and so finished with him, if he were dead and she had seen him buried in the earth and still and gone forever, if she could have been a widow and known her life with the man ended, it would have been easier for her. If the hamlet had known her widowed and if she could have kept before her pure and strong that true widowhood, and if she could have heard people say, when she passed or where she knew it said, "A very good true widow is that wife of Li, now dead. There he lies dead and buried and she goes steadfast and true to him, such a one as in the old days would have had a marble arch put up or at least an arch of stone for her honor." If she could have heard talk like this it would have been a strength to her and a thing to stay herself by, and to this shape that people made of her she might have set her heart and so lived better than she was because men thought her so.

But widow she was not, and often must she answer those who called to ask her how her man did and ever must she lie and cheerfully and keep him in constant mind through her very lies. They would call, "There you are, goodwife, and have you had a letter of late or message by some mouth to say how your man is?"

And she, passing by with a load for market across her shoulder or coming slowly home with empty baskets must answer often out of deathly weariness, "Yes, by word of mouth I hear he does right well, but he only writes me once a year."

But when she was come to her own house she was torn in two with all her lies. Sometimes she was filled with sadness and loneliness and she cried to her own heart, "How sorrowful and lone a woman am I whose only man is one I must make for myself out of words and lies!"

At such times she would sit and stare down the road and she would think heavily, "That blue robe of his would show a long way off, if he had a mind to turn to home again, so clear and fine a blue it was!"

And indeed if ever she saw a bit of blue anywhere in the distance her heart would leap, and if a man passed in the distance wearing a blue robe she could not but stop what she did and hold her breath to see how he came, shading her eyes against the sun if she were in the field, her hoe dropped from her hand, while she watched if he came this way or that or if he passed or if he went a long way off. And always it was not he who passed, for blue is a very common color and any man might wear a blue robe, if he be a poor and common man.

THE MOTHER

But there were times when her lies made her angry at
him and she told herself the man was not worth it and
if he had come home at one such time as this she would
have burst her anger full upon him and cursed him
soundly while she loved him because he made her suffer
so. Times there were when this deep anger lasted over
days, so that she was sullen and short with the children
and with the grandmother and pushed the dog away
roughly with her hoe, although she grieved her own
heart the more when she was so.

At one such time as this it came about that it was time
for the rice to be measured after harvest. Once more she
had struggled through the harvest and alone except for
such help as the lad could give, and a day or two from
the good cousin, and the day came for the division of the
threshed grain. It seemed to the woman that day as
though her longing and her anger had made her heart
like raw flesh, so that everything she saw fell on it
sorely as a blow, and things she did not see of common
times she saw and felt this day.

And while she longed, there upon her threshing-floor
beside the heaped grain the agent stood, the landlord's
agent, and he was a tall man dressed in a silk robe of
gray, and his face square and large and handsome in its
bold way. He had his old manner she remembered, a
manner of seeming courtesy, but his eyes were full and
the lids heavy and half closed over them, and the
woman knew from the way he stared at her from under

123

those heavy drooping lids that he had heard her tale and how her husband was gone out to other parts and never had come back. Yes, there was something today in her full heart that caught this knowledge in him, and the truth was he was such a man as could not look at any woman left alone and not wonder secretly what she was and how her heart was made and how her body was shaped. There was a dog's heart in him, for all his big, good frame and his square full face and his voice he made so hearty and frank. But in spite of his forced courtesy and his free words the tenants hated him, and they feared him because he had a high hard temper and this big body and two large, swift fists that he clenched and held hard against his thighs if any argued against what he said. Yes, and then he lifted the lids he drooped over his eyes, and his eyes were terrible, shining and black and cruel. Yet often they laughed at him, too, for if they gave him his fee without quarrel, he made a joke or two to salve the taking, and they could not but laugh at what he said, although with rue, for he had a way about him somehow.

So did he make a little merry on this day when he came to the mother's house where she lived alone without her man and he knew she did, and he called out heartily to the lad, "I see your mother does not need your father with such a man as you to tend the fields!"

Then the boy swaggered his little lean body and boasted, shy and bold at once, he was so pleased, "Oh, aye, I do my share," and he spat as he had seen men do, and set his arms upon his little bony thighs and felt himself grown and fully man.

Then the agent laughed and looked at the mother as though to laugh kindly with her over this lad of hers, and the woman could not but smile, and she handed him a bowl of tea she had poured out in common courtesy as to any passing guest. And being so near his laughing eyes she could not but look into them, and there was that great, greedy, starving heart of hers showing in her own eyes without her knowledge that it did. The man stared at her and scented her heat and he turned hot and grave and when he took the bowl he touched his hand to hers as though not knowing her hand was there. But the woman felt the touch and caught its meaning in her blood like flame.

Then she turned herself away shamed and would not hear what her own heart said. No, she busied herself with the grain and while she did it she grew suddenly afraid of her own self and she said to the lad in a low voice, "Run to our cousin and ask him to come hither and help me," and to her heart she said, to still its wildness, "If he is here—if our good cousin is here—"

But the lad was proud and wilful and he argued, "I am here, mother, and I will help you. What other do you need? See, I am here!"

Then the agent laughed loudly and slapped his thick thigh and he took secret advantage of the innocent lad and he cried, "So you are, my lad, and true enough your mother needs no other man!"

Then the lad grew the more bold being so encouraged and when his mother said again, half faintly, "It would be better if our cousin were here," the boy caught the faintness and he cried, "No, I will not call him, mother! I am man enough!" and he took up the scales and strutted to fill the measure with the grain and the woman laughed uneasily and let him be, and the truth was there was something in her, too, that pulled at her to let him be.

When the grain was measured out and she had made a measure full again to give the agent for himself, that agent put it from him in a lordly way and he smoothed his long straight upper lip and looking ardently into the woman's face—for who was there save these children and that old woman nodding in her sleep under the eaves by the door?—he said, "No, I will not have it! You are a lone woman now and your man gone from home and all this is your own labor. I will take no more of it than my landlord must have, or blame me if he does not. I will take no fee from you, goodwife."

Then was the woman suddenly afraid in the midst of the sweet sick heat that was upon her and she grew confused and pressed the fee upon him. But he would not have it. He pushed the measure away, his hand on hers while he did, and at last when he took the measure from her he poured the grain back into the basket where she kept it stored, and he would not have it.

Nor had she strength to beg him any more. Under this man's smooth face and smiling ways, under that gray costly robe of his, there was some strange and secret force that poured out of him into the shining autumn sun and clung to her and licked about her like a tongue of fire. She fell silent then and hung her head like any maid and when he poured the grain back and bowed and went his way, laughing and bowing and smoothing his long lip where there was no hair, she could not say a word. She stood there in silence, her bare brown feet thrust into broken shoes, one hand twisting the corner of her patched cotton coat.

When he was gone she lifted her head and looked after him and at that same instant he turned and caught her look and bowed and laughed again. Yet, in such a way he went, and afterwards she wished a thousand times she had not looked after him like that and yet she could not help it when she did it. Then the boy cried out gladly, "A good man, mother, not to take his fee! I never heard of such a good agent not to take his fee!" And when she went into the kitchen silently, half in a dream with what had passed, he following crying at her, "Is he not a good man, mother, who wanted nothing for himself?" And when still she answered nothing he cried peevishly, "Mother—mother!"

Then the mother started suddenly and she answered

in strange haste, "Oh—aye, son—" and the lad prattled on, "So good a man, mother—you see, he would take nothing from you at all, knowing how you are poor now that my father is gone."

But the mother stood still of a sudden, the lid of the cauldron lifted and still in her hand. She stared at the boy fixedly and her heart echoed strangely, shamed and yet filled with that sick sweet fever, "Did he want nothing of me?" Though to the lad she answered nothing.

Nor could the man forget the woman's heat. For this excuse and that he came back to the hamlet and now it was to make sure of some account which he thought he had written wrong, and now it was to complain that such a one had given a measure short and the landlord was angry with him. Most often of all he went to the cousin's house, which stood near the woman's, and he went to see of this and that, and now he brought some new seed of a kind of cotton that was held very fine in other parts or he brought a man with him carrying a load of lime or some such thing to make the fields more fertile, and the cousin was dazed with so much coming. At first he was afraid the agent had some evil purpose toward him and then he grew anxious when nothing came out for him to see, and he said to his wife, "It must be he has some very deep and evil purpose if it is so long leaking out of him," and he watched the man anxiously and sat and stared at him, yet impatient,

too, to be at his work again that waited for him, and yet
afraid to be lacking in courtesy to one who could do
him evil if he would.

But neither cousin nor cousin's wife saw how the
secret eyes of the agent went sliding under his lids toward
the woman across the way, and how if she were not
there upon her threshold, he stayed but a little while,
and how if she were there he sat on and on, facing her,
and often he cried in loud and false good nature, "No,
good fellow, I have no errand other than this. I am but
a common man, too, and I like nothing better than to
sit in an honest man's dooryard and feel the autumn
sun upon me." But all the while he stared across the
way where the woman sat spinning or sewing.

Now this was the season when the land was sinking
into quiescence for the winter. The wheat was planted
in the dry earth and waiting for a rain to sprout it, and
the mother took a little leisure and sat in her doorway
and mended the winter garments and made new shoes,
for the girl's sight was not enough for this, and never
would be. She sat there in the full sun for warmth, half
listening to the old woman's talk and what her children
had to say to her, and half dreaming, and her lips were
tranquil and her skin warm and golden brown with the
sun and her hair shiny black with health and newly
combed now she had the time to do it every day, and
these days she looked younger than she was, although
she was yet not thirty and five years old.

Well she knew that man sat there across the few feet of roadway but she would not look up and sometimes when she felt his look press her too hard she rose and went into the house and stayed there until she had seen him go. But she knew why he came and she knew he looked at her for a cause, and she could not forget him.

All through that winter she could not forget him somehow. At last it grew too cold for him to come even for his purpose. When the snow fell and when the winds came down bitter and dry out of the northwest, she might have forgotten him. But she did not.

Once more the new year came and she went into the town as she did every year and sold some grain and changed her silver into paper and she went and sought a different letter writer, and once more she had the letter written as though the man sent it, and once more the hamlet heard the news and knew she had the money from her man.

But this time their fresh envy and all their talk and praise put nothing in the woman's empty heart. Not even pride could comfort her this time. She listened to the letter read, her face quiet and cold, and she took it home and that night she put it in the oven with the burning grass. Then she went to the table in the room where there was a small drawer and after a while she opened it and brought out the three letters there, for so long had the man been gone now, and she took them also to the fire and laid them on the flames. The lad saw it, and he cried out astounded,

"Do you burn my father's letters then?"

"Aye," the mother answered, cold as death, her eyes on the quick flames.

"But how will we know where he is, then?" the lad wailed.

"I know as well as ever. Do you think I can forget?" the woman said.

So she emptied her heart clean.

But how can any heart live empty? On a day soon after this she went into the city to change again her bit of paper, for these days she did not trouble her cousin often, having learned to be alone, and when she had the ten pieces in her hand she turned to go and there a man stood by the door upon the street, and he stood smiling and smoothing his upper lip, and it was the landlord's agent.

Not since the late autumn had he seen her close as this, and there was none near who knew them and so he stared at her boldly and smiling and he said, "What do you here, goodwife?"

"I did but change a bit of money—" she broke off here, for she had been about to say on, "that my man sent me," but the words stuck in her throat somehow and she did not utter them.

131

"And what then?" he asked her, his lids lifted and his eyes pressing her.

She drooped her head and strove to speak as commonly she did, and she said, "I thought to go and buy a silver pin, or one washed with silver, to hold my hair. The one I had grew thin from long use and broke yesterday."

It was true her pin to hold her hair had so broken, and she said the truth before she knew it, and turned to go away, ashamed even before people who did not know her to be seen speaking to a man upon a town street, and he was a man somewhat notable in his looks, and being taller than most men and his face very square and pale, so that people were already looking at them curiously as they passed.

But the man followed behind her. She knew he followed behind her as she went soberly and modestly down the way and she was afraid not to do what she had said she would, and so she went to a small silver shop she knew and stood at the silversmith's counter and asked to see his pins of brass, washed with silver. And while she waited she toyed a moment with some silver earrings that were there and suddenly the agent came up while she toyed and he pretended he did not know her and he said to the silversmith, "How much are these earrings?"

Then the silversmith said, "I will weigh them to see

how much silver is there, and then will I sell them to you honestly and fairly by what they weigh."

And the silversmith let the pin wait a while, seeing this man was clad in silk and a better purchaser, doubtless, than this countrywoman in her blue cotton coat. So the woman could only stand and turn her head away from those bold secret eyes and the man stood indolently waiting as the silversmith put the rings upon the little scales.

"Two ounces and a half," the silversmith said in a loud voice. Then lowering his voice he added coaxingly, "But if you buy the earrings for your good lady, then why not add a pair of rings? Here are two to match the earrings, and it will all be a fine gift, suited to any woman's heart."

The man smiled at this and he said carelessly, "Add them, then." And then he said laughing, "But they are not for a wife—the wife I had died a six-month ago."

The silversmith made haste to add the rings, pleased at so fine a sale, and he said, "Then let them be for the new wife." But the man said no more but stood and stared and smoothed his lip. Not once did this man show he knew the countrywoman was there. He took the rings when they were wrapped and went away. But when he had turned his back the mother sighed and watched him half jealous for the one he had bought the trinkets for, such things as she would have loved and in her girlhood had often longed to have. And indeed

133

they were the very things she had said her husband bade her buy with the silver she spent, and the gossip often asked these days, "Where are those rings you said you have? Let me see what their pattern is." And the mother was often hard put to it and she said, "The silversmith is making them," or "I have put them in a certain place and I have forgot where they are for the moment," and many such excuses had she made until this last year when the gossip had said with how great malice, "And do you never wear those rings yet?" and then the mother answered, "I have not the heart and I will put them on the first day he comes home."

So when she had bought the pin and slipped it through her coil of hair, she turned home again thinking of the dainty silver things and she sighed and thought she had not heart to take her hard-earned silver and buy herself a toy, after all, seeing that doubtless it mattered to no one how she looked now, and she would let be as she was. Thinking thus and somewhat drearily, she wound her way out of the city gate and upon the narrow country road that branched off to the hamlet from the highway, and she thought of home and of the comfort of her food when she was there, the only comfort now her body had.

Suddenly out of the twilight of the short winter's evening there stood the man. Out of the twilight he stood, sudden and black, and he seized her wrist in his large soft hand and there was no other soul near by. No, it was the hour when countrymen are in their houses and it was cold and the air full of the night's frost and such a time as no one lingers out unless he must. Yet here was he, and he had her wrist and held it and she felt his hand on her and she stood still, smitten into stillness.

Then the man took the small parcel of silver he had and with his other hand he forced it into her hand that he held, and he closed her fingers over it and he said, "I bought these for none other than for you. For you alone I bought them. They are yours."

And he was gone into the gathering shade under the city wall, and there was she left alone, the silver trinkets in her hand.

Then she came to herself and she ran after him crying, "I cannot—but I cannot—."

But he was gone. Although she ran into the gate and peered through the flickering lights that fell from open shops, she could not see him. She was ashamed to run further into the town and look at this man's face and that in the dim light, and so she stood, uncertain and ashamed, until the soldiers who guarded the city gate called out in impatience, "Goodwife, if you are going out this gate tonight go you must because the hour is come when we must close it fast against the communists, those new robbers we have these days."

She went her way then once more and crossed the little hill and down into the valley, and after a while she thrust the trinkets in her bosom. The moon rose huge and cold and glittering as soon as the sun was set, and when she came home the children were in their bed, and the old grandmother asleep. Only the lad lay still awake and he cried when his mother came, "I was afraid for you, my mother, and I would have come to find you, only I was afraid to leave the children and my grandmother."

But she could not even smile at his so calling the other two children as though he were a man beside them. She answered, "Aye, here I be, at last, and very weary somehow," and she went and fetched a little food and ate it cold, and all the time the trinkets lay in her bosom.

When she had eaten she glanced toward the bed and by the candlelight she saw the lad slept too, and so she fastened the curtains and then she sat down beside the table and took the little packet from her breast and opened the soft paper which enwrapped it. There the rings lay, glittering and white, and the earrings were beautiful. Upon each were fastened three small fine chains, and at the end of each chain hung a little toy. She took them in her hard fingers and looked closely and upon one chain hung a tiny fish and upon the second a little bell and upon the third a little pointed star, all daintily and cleverly made and pleasing to any woman. She had never held such pretty things before in her hard brown palm. She sat and looked at them a while and sighed and wrapped them up again, not knowing what to do with them, or how to give them back to that man.

But when she had crept under the quilt with the children she could not sleep. Although her body was cold with the damp chill of the night her cheeks were burning hot and she could not sleep for a long time and then at last but lightly. And partly she dreamed of some strange thing shining, and partly she dreamed of a man's hot hand upon her.

X

SHE did not see the man again through the whole spring, although she remembered him. She did not see him until a day in the early summer, when the wheat was turning faintly gold, and she had sown her rice in beds for seedlings, and it was sprouted new and green and set in small blocks of jade near the house where it could be well watched by the old grandmother against the greedy birds that loved its tenderness. And all this time her heart lay in her hot and fallow.

But there came a day in that early summer, a day windless and full of soft new heat. The cicadas called their sharp loves and when they had called past the crisis their voices trailed slow and languorous into silence again. Into the valley the sun poured down its heat like clear warm wine and the smooth warm stones of the solitary street of the little hamlet threw back the heat again so that the air shimmered and danced above them, and through those waves the little naked children ran and played, their smooth bodies shining with their sweat.

There was no little passing wind of any sort at all. Standing upon her threshold the mother thought she had never felt such close and sudden heat as this so soon in summer. The younger boy ran to the edge of the pool and sat in the water there, laughing and shouting to his playmates to come and join him, and the elder lad took off his coat and rolled his trousers high and put on his head a wide old bamboo hat that had been his father's once and went out to the field of newly sprouted corn. The girl sat in the house for darkness and her mother heard her sighing there. Only the old woman loved this heat and she sat in the sun and slipped the coat from her old withered frame and let the sun soak down into her old bones and on her breasts that hung like bits of dried skin on her bosom, and she piped when she saw her son's wife there, "I never fear to die in summer, daughter! The sun is good as new blood and bones to an old dried thing like me!"

But the mother could not bear the outer heat. Heat there was enough inside her and her blood seemed this day to thunder through her veins with too much heat. She left the house then saying, "I must go and water the rice a while. A very drying sun today, old mother," and she took her hoe and on her shoulder slung her empty water buckets and so walked down the narrow path to where a further pond lay somewhat higher than the seed beds of the rice, and she walked gratefully, because the air though hot was not so shut and lifeless as it had been on the street.

She walked on and met no one at all, because it was the hour after noon when men take their rest. Here and there if a man had gone early to his field he sought the shade, for, after all, the heat was too great for labor, and he lay sleeping under some tree, his hat covering his face against the flies, and beside him stood his beast, its head drooping and all its body slack with heat and drowsiness. But the mother could bear the heat because it came down out of the sky and was not shut between walls or all in her own veins.

She worked on a while then in her seed beds and with her hoe she cut a little gate in the higher edge of the bed and she dug a small water way to the pond, and then she went to the pond's edge and with her buckets slung upon the pole she dipped first one and then the other into the water and then emptied them into the ditch she had dug. Over and over she dipped the water and watched the earth grow dark and moist and it seemed to her she fed some thirsting living thing and gave it life.

Now while she was at this task she straightened her back once and set her buckets down and went and sat upon the green edge of the pond to rest, and as she sat she looked to the north where the hamlet was and there she saw a man stop and ask the old woman something and then he turned and came toward her where she sat by this pond. She looked as he came and knew him. It was the landlord's agent, and while he came she remembered she had his trinkets still and she hung her head not knowing how to speak of them without giving them back again, and not daring now to go and find them and give them back to him in this full light of day when any passing soul might see her do it and the old woman wide awake, too, in the sun, and she was quick to see a thing she ought not.

So the man came on, and when he was come the mother rose slowly, being lesser in place than he and woman, too, before a man. But he called out freely and he said, "Goodwife, I came but to look and see what the wheat is this year and guess the harvest from the fields!"

But while he spoke his eyes ran up and down her body, clad for the heat in but a single coat and trousers of patched blue stuff worn thin and close to her shape and his eyes fixed themselves upon her bare brown feet and in fear of her own heart she muttered rudely, "The fields lie yonder—look then, and see!"

So he glanced over them from where he stood and he said in his pleasant, townsman's way, "Very fair fields, goodwife, and there have been worse harvests than there will be this year." And he took out a little folded book and wrote something down on it with a sort of stick she had never seen before, seeing he needed not to dip it in ink at all, as the letter writer did, for it came out black itself. She watched him write and half it made her curious and half it touched her and made her proud to think so learned and goodly a man had looked at one like her, even when he should not, and she thought she would not speak of the trinkets this one time.

When he had finished his writing he said to her smiling and smoothing his lip, "If you have time, show me that other field of yours that stands in barley, for I ever do forget which is yours and which your cousin's."

"Mine is there around the hill," she said half unwillingly, and now her eyes were dropped and she made as if to take the hoe again.

"Around the hill?" the man said and then his voice grew soft and he smoothed that lip of his with his big soft hand and smiled and said, "But show me, goodwife!"

He fixed his eyes on her steadily now and openly and his gaze had power to move her somehow and she put down her hoe and went with him, following after him as women do when they walk with men.

The sun beat down on them as they went and the earth was warm beneath their feet and green and soft with grass. Suddenly as she walked the woman felt her blood grow all sweet and languorous in her with the hot sun. And without knowing why, it gave her some deep pleasure to look at the man who walked ahead of her, at his strong pale neck, shining with sweat, at his body moving in the long smooth robe of summer stuff, at his feet in white clean hose and black shoes of cloth. And she went silently on her bare feet and she came near to him and caught some fragrance from him, too strong for perfume, some compound of man's blood and flesh and sweat. When she caught it in her nostrils she was stirred with longing and it was such a longing she grew frightened of herself and of what she might do, and she cried out faltering, and standing still upon the grassy path, "I have forgot something for my old mother!" and when he turned and looked at her, she faltered out again thickly, her whole body suddenly hot and weak, "I have forgot a thing I had to do—" and she turned from him and walked as quickly as she could and left him there staring after her.

Straight she went to her house and she crept across the threshold and none noticed her, for everyone lay sleeping. The heat of the day had grown heavier as the afternoon wore on. Across the way the cousin's wife sat sleeping, her mouth ajar, and the last babe sleeping at her breast. Here the old grandmother slept too, her head drooped and her nose upon her chin, and her clothes slipped to her waist still as she had sat in the sun. The girl had come out of the close room and lay curled against a cool stone for a pillow and she slept, and the younger lad lay naked and stretched to his full length beneath the willow tree, asleep.

The very day had changed. It was grown darker and more still and full of deeper and more burning heat. Great clouds loomed swollen, black and monstrous, up from the hills. But they shone silver-edged, luminous from some strange inner light. Even the sound of any insect, the call of any bird, was stilled in the vast hot silence of that day.

But the mother was far from sleep. She went softly into the darkened, silent room, and she sat herself upon the bed and the blood thundered in her ears, the blood of her strong hungry body. Now she knew what was amiss with her. She pretended nothing to herself now, as a townswoman might pretend, that there was some illness she had. No, she was too simple to pretend when well she knew how it was with her, and she was more frightened than she had ever been in her whole life, for she knew that such hunger as was in her now grew raving if it were not fed. . . . She did not even dream she could repulse him, now she knew her own hunger was the same as his, and she groaned aloud and cried to her heart, "It would be better if he would not have me— Oh, I wish he would not have me, and that I might be saved!"

But even while she groaned she rose driven from off that bed and went from the sleeping hamlet and to the fields along the way that she had come. She walked along under the great, black, bright-edged clouds and about her were the hills, livid green and clean against the blackness. She went under such a sky, along the little winding turn the path took where it turned past a small and ruined shrine, and there in the door of the shrine the man stood, waiting.

And she could not pass him. No, when he went inside and waited she followed to the door and looked and there he stood inside the twilight of the windowless shrine, waiting, and his eyes gleamed out of that twilight, shining as a beast's eyes, waiting, and she went in.

They looked at each other in the dim light, two people in a dream, desperate, beyond any power now to stay, and they made ready for what they must do.

Yet did the woman stop once, too. She looked up from her dream and she saw the three gods in the shrine, the chief a staid old man staring straight ahead of him, and by his side two small attendants, little, decent gods of the wayside for those who paused in their journey for worship or for shelter. She took the garment she had laid aside and went and threw it on their heads and covered up their staring eyes.

XI

IN the night of that same day the wind rose suddenly
as a tiger's roar out of the distant hills, and it blew
the clouds down out of the sky where they had
hung heavy and full of rain, their light long gone. And
the sudden rains poured and washed the heats out of
that day. When at last the mist was gone, the dawn,
pure and cool, grew quiet and fell from a gray and
tranquil sky.

Now out of that storm and chill came down from
heaven suddenly, at last, the old woman's death. She had
sat asleep too long, her old body naked for the wind to
blow upon when the sun went down, and when the
mother came home at twilight, silent, and as if she came
from the field and honest labor, she found the old
woman in her bed and cold with sudden chills and aches
and she cried out, "Some wicked spirit has caught me,
daughter! Some ill wind fell on me!" And she moaned
and put out her little shriveled hand and the mother took
it and it was dry and burning hot.

Almost was the mother glad to have it so. Almost did
she rejoice there was this thing to take her mind from
her own heart and from the sweet and evil thing that

she had done that day. She murmured, "It was an ill black sky—very nearly I came home to see if you sat under such a sullen sky, but I thought you would see its hue and come in from under it."

"I slept, though," the old woman wailed, "I slept, and I slept on and we all slept, and when I woke the sun was gone and I was cold as death."

Then the mother hastened and made hot water for the old woman and put some ginger in it and hot herbs and the old woman drank it. Yet in the night her dry fever grew and she complained she could not breathe because some imp sat on her chest and drove his knife into her lungs, and after a while she ceased talking and lay breathing roughly from her pressed lungs.

And the mother was glad she must not sleep. Through the night she was glad she must sit beside the old woman's bed and watch her and give her water when she moaned for it and put the quilt about her when she pushed it off and cried that she burned and yet shivered too. Outside the night had grown black and mighty rains poured down upon the thatched roof and here and there it broke through and leaked, so that the mother must drag the old woman's bed out from its corner where the rain seeped in, and over the bed where the children slept she laid a reed mat to hold the leaks off. Yet all these things she was glad to have to do and glad to be so busy all night long.

When the morning came the old soul was worse. Yes,

any eye could see it, and the mother sent the lad for the cousin and he came and the cousin's wife came and this neighbor and that and they all looked at the old woman who lay now only partly knowing what was about her, and partly dazed with her fever and the pain she had when she breathed. Each one cried out what must be done and what remedy could be tried, and the mother hastened here and there to try them all in turn. Once the old woman came to herself and seeing the crowd gathered there, she panted from her laden breast, "There is an imp sits here on me and holds me down. . . . My hour—my hour—"

Then the mother hastened to her and she saw there was a thing the old soul had to say and could not get it out, but she plucked trembling at the shroud she wore that was full of patches now, and she had laughed when every patch was set in place and cried she would outlive the garment yet. But now she plucked at it and the mother bent her head low and the old woman gasped, "This shroud—all patched—my son—"

The crowd stared to hear these words and looked wondering at each other, but the elder lad said quickly, "I know what she wants, mother. She wants her third shroud new to lie in, the one my father said he would send, and she ever said she would outlive this one she has now."

The old woman's face lit faintly then and they all cried out who heard it, "How stout an old soul is this!"

THE MOTHER

and they said, "Well, here is a very curious brave old woman, and she will have her third shroud as she ever said she would!"

And some dim, dying merriment came on the old woman's owlish sunken face and she gasped once more, "I will not die till it is made and on—"

In greatest haste then was the stuff bought, and the cousin went to buy it and the mother told him, "Buy the very best you can of stout red cotton stuff and to-morrow I will pay you if you have the silver by you now." For she had determined that the old woman would have the very best, and that night when the house was still she dug into the earth and got the silver out that she had hid there and she took out what was needful to send the old mother to her death content.

And indeed, it seemed as if the thing she would not think of now, the memory of an hour she drove into her secret places, busying herself and glad to be so busy, it seemed as if this waiting memory made her kind and eager to be spent for these who were hers. Somehow it eased her of that secret hour to do her scrupulous best now. For these two nights she slept none at all, wearying herself eagerly, nor was she ever angry at the children, and she was most gentle to the old and dying woman. When the cousin fetched the cloth she held it to the old dying eyes and she said, speaking loudly now, for the old woman grew deaf and blind more quickly every hour, "Hold hard, old mother, till I have it made!"

THE MOTHER

And the old soul said, bravely, "Aye—I will not die!" though she had not breath for any speech now and scarcely any breath at all, so that every one she drew came screeching through her lungs pitifully, very hard to draw.

Then the mother made haste with her needle, and she made the garments of the bright good stuff, red as a bride's coat, and the old woman lay watching her, her dim eyes fixed upon the stuff where it glowed in the mother's lap. She could not eat now or swallow any food or drink, not even the warm human milk one kindly woman milked from her own breast with a bowl, since sometimes this good milk will save an old dying man or woman. She clung but to this scanty bit of air, waiting.

And the mother sewed and sewed, and the neighbors brought in food so that she need not stop for anything but could sew on. In one day and a part of the night it was done, and the cousin and the cousin's wife stood by to see it and a neighbor or two, and indeed the whole hamlet did not sleep, but stayed awake to wonder if the mother would win that race, or death.

But it was done at last, the scarlet burial robes were done, and the cousin lifted the old body and the mother and the cousin's wife drew on the fine new garments on the old and withered limbs, brown now and dry as old sticks of some dead tree. But the old soul knew when it was finished. Speak she could not, but she lay and drew one last rattling breath or two, and opened wide her eyes and smiled her toothless smile, knowing she had lived through to her third shroud, which was her whole desire, and so she died triumphantly.

Yet when the burial day was over and the need for being busy was past, still the mother busied herself. She labored as she never had upon the land and when the lad would do a thing she had begun she cried roughly, "Let me do it—I miss the old mother sorely and more sorely than I thought I could, and I blame myself that I did not go home that day and see if she were warm when the storm came up and covered the sun."

And she let it be thought through the hamlet that she sorrowed for the old woman gone, and blamed herself, and many praised her for her sorrow and said, "How good a daughter-in-law to mourn like this!" And they comforted her and said, "Do not mourn so, goodwife. She was very old and her life ended, and when the hour is come that has been set for each of us before ever we can walk or talk, then what need of mourning? You have your man alive yet, and you have your two sons. Take heart, goodwife."

But it was an ease to her too to have every cause to cover up her fear and melancholy. For she had cause to be afraid, and she had time now, even while she worked upon her land, to take out of her heart that fear which had been hiding there ever since the hour in the rising storm. Glad she was all these days that she had been in such haste, glad even for the old woman's death, and to herself she thought most heavily, "It is better that the old soul is dead and cannot know what is to come if it must come."

One month passed and she was afraid. Two months passed and three and harvest came, the grain was threshed, and what had been fear beneath her labor day by day was now a certainty. There was no more to doubt and she knew the worst had befallen her, mother of sons, goodwife honored in her hamlet, and she cursed the day of the storm and her own foolish heats. Well she might have known that with her own body all hot and open and waiting as it had been, her mind all eaten up with one hunger, well she might have known it was such a moment as must bear fruit. And the man's body, too, so strong and good and full of its own power— how had she ever dreamed it could be otherwise?

Here was strange motherhood now that must be so secret and watched with such dismay in the loneliness of the night while the children slept. And however she might be sickened she dared not show it. Strange it was that when she bore her proper children she was not sick at all, but now her food turned on her when she ate a mouthful. It was as though this seed in her was so strong and lusty that it grew like a foul weed in her, doing what it would with her body ruthlessly, and she could not let a sign of it be seen.

Night after night she sat up in her bed, too ill at ease to lie down, and she groaned within herself, "I wish I were alone again and had not this thing here in me —I wish I were alone again as I was, and I would be content—" and it came to her often and wildly that she would hang herself there upon the bedpost. But yet she could not. There were her own good children, and she looked upon their sleeping faces and she could not, and she could not bear to think of the neighbors' looks on her dead body when they searched her for her cause of death. There was nothing then save that she must live on.

Yet in spite of all this pain the woman was not healed of her desire toward that townsman, though she often hated while she longed for him. Rather did it seem he held her fast now by this secret hold that grew within her. She had repented that she ever yielded to him and yet she yearned for him often day and night. In the midst of her true shame and all her wishing she had withstood him, she yearned for him still. Yet she was ashamed to seek him out, and fearful too lest she be seen, and she could only wait again until he came, because it seemed to her if she went and sought him then she was lost indeed, and after that stuff for any man to use.

But here was a strange thing. The man was finished with her. He came no more throughout that whole summer until the grain was reaped when he must come, and he came hard and quarrelsome as he used to be and he took his full measure of his grain so that the lad cried wondering, "How have we made him angry, mother, who was so kind to us last year?"

And the woman answered sullenly, "How can I know?" But she knew. When he would not look at her, she knew.

Not even on the day of harvest feasting would he look at her, although she washed herself freshly and combed her hair and smoothed it down with oil and put on a clean coat and trousers and her one pair of stockings and the shoes she had made for the old woman's burial day. So garbed and her cheeks red with sick hope and shyness and her eyes bright with all her desperate secret fears, she hurried here and there busying herself before his eyes about the feast, and she spoke to this one and to that, forcing herself to be loud and merry. The women stared astonished at her flaming cheeks and glittering eyes and at her loud voice and laughter, she who used to be so quiet where men were.

But for all this the man did not look at her. He drank of the new wine made of rice and as he tasted it he cried loudly to the farmers, "I will have a jug or two of that for myself, if you can spare it, farmers, and set the clay seal on well and sound to keep it sweet." But he never looked at her, or if she came before him his eyes passed over her as they might over any common country wife whose name he did not know.

Then the woman could not bear it. Yes, although

she knew she should be glad he did not want her any more, she could not bear it. She went home in the middle of that day of feasting and she searched from out their secret place those trinkets he had given her once and she was trembling while she searched. She hung the rings in her ears, taking out the little wires she had worn there all these years to keep the holes open, and she pushed the rings over her hard strong fingers, and once more she made a chance to see him, standing on the edge of the feast where women stood to serve the men who ate. There the gossip sat among them, gay for the day in her new shoes, and her feet thrust out to show them off, and she cried out, "Well, goodwife, there you are and you did buy your trinkets after all and wear them too, although your man is still away!"

She cried so loudly that all the women turned to look and laugh and the men even turned to see and smile a little, too, at the women's merriment. Then the agent, hearing the laughter and the witty sayings that arose against the woman, looked up carelessly and haughtily from his bowl, his jaws moving as he looked, for his mouth was full of food, and he said carelessly and loud enough for her to hear, "What woman is it?" And his eyes fell on her scarlet face and he looked away as if he had never known her and fell to his bowl again. And the woman, feeling the scarlet draining from her face too fast, crept out and ran away and they laughed to see her run for shame at all their merriment.

THE MOTHER

From that day on the mother kept out of the way of others and she stayed alone with her children, and hid the growing of the wild thing within her. Yet she pondered day and night what she could do. Outwardly she worked as she ever had, storing the grain and setting all in order for the winter, and when the festival of midautumn came and the hamlet feasted and each house had its own joy and the little street was merry with the pleasure and rejoicing and the houses full of grain and food, the mother, though she had no joy, yet made a few small moon cakes for her own children, too. When the moon rose on the night of the feast, they ate the cakes upon the threshing-floor and under the willow trees and saw the full moon shining down as bright as any sun almost.

But they ate gravely and it seemed the children felt their own lack and the mother's lack of joy, and at last the eldest said, solemnly, "Sometimes I think my father must be dead because he never comes."

The mother started then and said quickly, "Evil son you be to speak of such a thing as your own father's death!"

But a thought had come to her.

And the lad said again, "Sometimes I think I will start forth seeking for him. I might go when the wheat is sown this year, if you will give me a little silver, and I can tie my winter clothes upon my back, if it be I am delayed in finding him."

Then the mother grew afraid and she cried to turn

his mind away, "Eat another little cake, my son, and wait another year or so. What would I do if you went away and did not come back either? Wait until the younger son is large enough to fill your place."

But the younger son cried stoutly, being wilful always when he had a wish to make, "But if my brother goes, I will go too," and he set his little red lips pouting and he stared angrily at his mother. Then the mother said reproachfully to the eldest, "There—you see what you do when you say such things and set his mind on wandering!" And she would not hear any more of it.

But the thought clung in her mind, and afterwards she pondered on it. Here was she alone now these five years. Five years—and would not a man have come long since if he were coming? Five years gone—and he must be dead. It must be she was widow, perhaps a widow years long, and never knew it. And the landlord's agent was not wed. She was widow and he not wed, for she had heard him say that his wife was dead last year but she had not heeded, for what was it to her then, who was not widow? Yes, she must be widow. That night she watched the great moon set high in the heavens and she watched far into the night, the children sleeping and all the hamlet sleeping save a dog here and there barking at the enormous moon, and more and more it seemed to her she must be widow, and if she were—if she were wed as soon as he would say, would it be soon enough?

And in the strangest way the thing hastened upon her.

The lad would not forget his plan and he worked fever-
ishly to plough the fields and sow the wheat and when it
was done he would have set out that very day to find
his father. Tall the lad was now as his father had been
almost, and lean and hard as bamboo and as supple, and
no longer any little child to bear refusal and he was quiet
and stubborn in his nature, never forgetting a plan he
made, and he said, "Let me go now and see where my
father is—give me the name of the city where he lives
and the house where he works!"

Then in despair the mother said to put him off, "But
I burned those letters and now must we wait until the
new year comes when he will send another."

And he cried, "Yes, but you said you knew!"

And she said hastily, "So I thought I did, but what
with this and that and the old mother's dying, I have
forgot again, and I know I have forgot, because when
she lay dying, I would have sent a letter to him and I
could not because I had forgot." And when he looked
at her reproachfully, scarcely believing her, she cried
out angrily, "And how did I know you would want to go
and leave it all on me now when you are just old enough
to be some worth? I never dreamed that you would
leave your mother, and I know a letter will come at the
new year as it always has."

So the lad could but put aside his wish then for the
time and he waited in his sullen humor, for he had set
his heart to see his father. Scarcely could he remember

him, but he seemed to remember him as a goodly merry man and the lad longed after him for in these days he did not love his mother well because she seemed always out of temper with him and not understanding of any speech, and he longed for his father.

At last the mother did not know what to do, except that something she must do and quickly, for even if the letter was not written at new year time, the lad would worry at her and sooner or later she must tell him all the truth and how would she ever make him see how what had been a little lie at first to save her pride as woman, had grown great and firm now with its roots in years, and very hard to change?

And then she tried to comfort herself again, and to say the man must be dead. Whoever heard of any man who would not come back sometimes to his land and his sons and his old home, if he yet lived? He was dead. She was sure he was dead, and so saying many times, sureness came into her heart and she believed him dead and there was needed but an outward sign to satisfy the lad and those who were in the hamlet.

Once more she went into the town then on this old task, and she went and sought a new letter writer this time, whom she had never seen before, and she sighed and said, "Write to my brother's wife and say her husband is dead. And how did he die? He was caught in a burning house, for the house where he lived caught on fire from a lamp turned over by some slave, and there he burned up in his sleep and even his ashes are lost so there is no body to send home."

And the letter writer wrote her own name for the sister's name and she gave a false name as of some stranger who wrote to tell the news and for a little more he wrote the name of some other town than this, and he scented something strange here, but he let it pass, too, since it was none of his affair and he had silver here to pay for silence.

So was the woman saved. But she could not wait to finish her salvation. No, she must let the landlord's agent know somehow, and she went here and there and asked where the landlord's old home was, where he did not live now but where the agent doubtless was well known. And she grew heedless in her anxiety to be saved, and she ran there and it seemed the gods were with her on that day and aided her, for there he came alone and she met him at the gate of the house and as he was ready to turn in to it. Then she cried out and laid her hand upon his arm, and he looked down at her and at her hand upon his arm and he said, "What is it, woman?"

And she whispered, "Sir, I am widowed—I have but heard this day I am widowed!"

And he shook her hand off and he said loudly, "What is that to me!" And when she looked at him painfully he said roughly, "I paid you—I paid you very well!" And suddenly someone he knew called out from the street and laughed and said, "How now, good fellow? And a very pretty, lusty goodwife, too, to lay hold on a man thus!"

But the man called back, scarcely lifting those heavy lids of his, and he said coldly, "Aye—if you like them coarse and brown, but I do not!" And he went on his way.

She stood there then astonished and ashamed and understanding nothing. But how had she been paid? What had he ever given her? And suddenly she remembered the trinkets he had given her. That was her pay! Yes, by those small worthless trinkets he held himself free of all that he had done.

What could she do, then, knowing all? She set her feet steadfastly upon the road to home, her heart deathly still within her, and she said over and over, "It is not time to weep yet—the hour is not come yet when I may weep." And she would not let her weeping come. No, the weeping gathered in her great and tremulous but she would not weep. She held her heart hard and silent for a day or two, until the news came, the letter she had written, and she took it to the reader in the hamlet, and she said steadily as she gave it to him, "I fear there is ill news in it, uncle—it is come out of time."

Then the old man took it and he read it and started and he cried, "It is bad news, goodwife—be ready!"

"Is he ill?" she said in her same steady way.

And the old man laid the letter down and took the

spectacles from his eyes and he answered solemnly, staring at her, "Dead!"

Then the mother threw her apron over her head and she wept. Yes, she could weep now and she wept, safely, and she wept on and on as though she knew him truly dead. She wept for all her lonely years and because her life had been so warped and lone and she wept because her destiny had been so ill and the man gone, and she wept because she dared not bear this child she had in her, and last she wept because she was a woman scorned. All the weeping she had been afraid to do lest child hear her or neighbor, now she could weep out and none need know how many were the sorrows that she wept.

The women of the hamlet came running out to comfort her when they heard the news and they comforted her and cried out she must not fall ill with weeping, for there were her children still and the two good sons, and they went and fetched the sons and led them to her for comfort, and the two lads stood there, the eldest silent, pale as though in sudden illness, and the youngest bellowing because his mother wept.

Suddenly in the midst of the confusion a loud howl arose and a noisier weeping than the mother's, and it was the gossip's, who was suddenly overcome with all the sorrow roundabout her, and the great oily tears ran down her cheeks and she sobbed loudly, "Look at me, poor soul —I am worse off than you, for I have no son at all—not one! I am more piteous than you, goodwife, and worse than any woman I ever saw for sorrow!" And her old sorrow came up in her so fresh and new that all the women were astonished and they turned to comfort her, and in the midst of the fray the mother went home, her two sons after her, weeping silently as she went, for she could not stay her weeping. Yes, she sat herself down and wept at her own door, and the elder lad wept silently a little too, now, wiping his eyes with the back of his hand, and the little boy wept on, not understanding what it meant to have his father dead, since he could not remember what the father was, and the girl wept and pressed her hands against her eyes and moaned softly and she said, "I must weep because my father is dead— my tears burn me so—yet must I weep for my dead father!"

But the mother could not weep to any end, and she knew she could not until she had done what she must do. So for the time she ceased her weeping and comforted them somewhat with her own silence while she thought what she would do.

She would have said there was no path for her to turn, unless to death, but there was one way, and it was to tear from out her body this greedy life she felt there growing. But she could not do it all alone. There must be one to aid her, and there was none to turn to save her cousin's wife. Much the mother wished she need not tell a soul what she must do, and yet she did not know how to do it alone. And the cousin's wife was a coarse good creature, too, one who knew the earth and the ways of men and knew full well the earthy body of a woman that is fertile and must bear somehow. But how to tell her?

Yet the thing came easily enough, for in a day or so thereafter when the two women stood alone upon a pathway talking, having met by some small accident or other, the cousin's wife said in her loud and kindly way, "Cousin, eat and let your sorrowing cease, for I do swear your face is as yellow as though you had worms in you."

And the thought rose in the mother's mind and she said it, low and bitterly, "So I have a worm in me, too, that eats my life out."

And when the cousin's wife stared, the mother put her hand to her belly and she said, halting, "Something does grow in me, cousin, but I do not know what it can be unless it is an evil wind of some sort."

Then the cousin's wife said, "Let me see it," and the mother opened her coat and the cousin's wife felt her where she had begun to swell, and she said astonished, "Why, cousin, it is like a child there, and if you had a husband, I would say that it was so with you!"

Then the mother said nothing but she hung her head miserably and could not lift her eyes, and the cousin saw a stirring in her belly and she cried out in a terror, "It is a child, I swear, yet how can it be except it be conceived by spirit, since your man is gone these many years? But I have heard it said it does happen sometimes to women and in olden times it happened often, if they were of a saintly sort, that gods came down and visited them. Yet you be no great saint, cousin, a very good woman, it is true, and held in good respect, but still angry and sudden sometimes and of a lusty temper. But have you felt a god about?"

Then the mother would like to have told another lie and she longed to say she did feel a god one day when she stood in the wayside shrine to shelter in a storm, but when she opened her lips to shape the lie she could not. Partly she was afraid to lie so blackly about the old decent god there whose face she covered, and partly she was so weary now she could lie no more. So she lifted her head and looked miserably at the cousin's wife and the red flowed into her pale cheeks and spotted them; she would have given half her life now if she could have told a full deceiving lie. But she could not and there it was. And the good woman who looked at her saw how it was and she asked no question nor how it came about, but she said only, "Cover yourself, sister, lest you be cold."

And the two walked on a while and at last the mother said in a very passion of bitterness, "It does not matter who begot it and none shall ever know and if you will help me through this, cousin and my sister, I will care for you as long as my life is in me."

And the cousin's wife said in a low voice, "I have not

lived so many years as I have and never seen a woman rid herself of a thing she did not want."

And for the first time the mother saw a hope before her and she whispered, "But how—but how—" and the cousin's wife said, "There are simples to be bought if one has the money, strong stuff that kills woman and child sometimes, and always it is harder than a birth, but if you take enough, it will do."

And the mother said, "Then let it kill me, if it will only kill this thing, and so save my sons and these others the knowledge."

Then the cousin's wife looked steadfastly at the mother and she stopped where she was and looked at her, and she said, "Yes, cousin, but will it come about again like this, now that your man is dead?"

Then did the mother swear and she cried in agony, "No, and I will throw myself into the pond and cool myself forever if it comes on me hot again as it did in the summer."

That night she dug out from the ground a good half of her store of silver and when the chance came she gave it to the cousin's wife to buy the simples.

On a night when all was bought and the stuff brewed, the cousin's wife came in the darkness and she whispered to the waiting woman, "Where will you drink it? For it cannot be done in any house, being so bloody a business as it is."

Then the mother remembered that wayside shrine and

how lonely it was with so few wayfarers passing by, and none in the night, and to that wayside shrine the two women went, and the mother drank the brew and she lay down upon the ground, and waited.

Presently in the deep night the stuff seized on her with such gripes as she never dreamed of and she gave herself up to die. And as the agony went on she came at last to forget all except the agony, and she grew dazed with it. Yet in the midst of it she remembered not to scream to ease herself, nor did they dare to light a torch or any little light, lest any might by some strange chance pass and see from even a distance an unaccustomed light in that shrine.

No, the mother must suffer on as best she could. The sweat poured down her body like rain and she was dead to everything except the fearful griping, as though some beast laid hold on her to tear the very vitals from her, and at last it seemed a moment came when they were torn from her indeed, and she gave one cry.

Then the cousin's wife came forward with a mat she had, and took what was to be taken, and she felt and whispered sadly, "It would have been a boy, too. You are a fortunate mother who have so many sons in you."

But the mother groaned and said, "There never will be another now."

Then she lay back and rested on the ground a little and when she could they went back to the house, she leaning on the kindly cousin's arm and holding back her moans. And when they passed a pond, the cousin threw the roll of matting into it.

For many days thereafter the mother lay ill and weak upon her bed, and the good cousin aided her in what way she could, but she lay ill and half-sick the winter through that year so that to lift a load and carry it to market was a torture and yet she must do it now and then. At last, though, she rose sometimes more easily on a fair day and sat a while in the sun. So spring came on and she grew somewhat better, but still not herself, and often when the cousin brought some dainty dish to coax her she would press her hand to her breast and say, "It seems I cannot swallow. There is something heavy here. My heart hangs here between my breasts so heavy and full I cannot swallow. My heart seems full of pain I cannot weep away. If I could weep once to the end I would be well again."

So it seemed to her. But she could not weep. All spring she could not weep nor could she work as she was used, and the elder son struggled to do what must be done, and the cousin helped more than he was able. And the mother could not weep or work.

So it was until a certain day came when the barley was bearded, and she sat out in the sun listlessly, her hair not combed that morning she was so weary. Suddenly there was the sound of a step, and when she looked up that landlord's agent stood. When the elder son saw him he came forward and he said, "Sir, my father is dead now and I stand in his place, for my mother has been ill these many months. I must go with you now to guess the harvest, if you have come for that, for she is not able."

Then the man, this townsman, this smooth-haired, smooth-lipped man, looked at the mother full and carelessly and well he knew what had befallen her, and she knew he knew and she hung her head in silence. But the man said carelessly, "Come then, lad," and the two went away and left her there alone.

Now well she knew she had no hope from this man. Nor did she want him any more, her body had been weak so long. But this last sight of him was the last touch she needed. She felt the lump she called her heart melt somehow and the tears rushed to her eyes, and she rose and walked by a little unused path across the land to a rude lonely grave she knew, the grave of some unknown man or woman, so old none knew whose it was now, and she sat there on the grassy mound and waited. And at last she wept.

First her tears came slow and bitter but freely after a while and then she laid her head against the grave and wept in the way that women do when their hearts are too full with sorrow of their life and spilled and running over and they care no more except they must be eased somehow because all of life is too heavy for them. And the sound of her weeping reached the little hamlet even,

THE MOTHER

borne on the winds of spring, and hearing it the mothers
in the houses and the wives looked at each other and
they said softly, "Let her weep, poor soul, and ease herself. She has not been eased these many months of
widowhood. Tell her children to let her weep."
And so they let her weep.

But after long weeping the mother heard a sound, a
soft rustling there beside her, and looking up in the
twilight, for she had wept until the sun was set, there
came her daughter, feeling her way over the rough
ground and she cried as she came, "Oh, mother, my
cousin's wife said let you weep until you eased yourself,
but are you not eased yet with so much weeping?"
Then was the mother roused. She was roused and she
looked at the child and sighed and she sat up and
smoothed back her loosened hair and wiped her swollen
eyes and rose and the child put out her hand and felt for
her mother's hand, shutting her eyes against the shining
evening glow that was rosy where the sun went down,
and she said plaintively, "I wish I never had to weep, for
when I weep, my tears do burn me so!"
At these few words the mother came to herself, suddenly washed clean. Yes, these few words, spoken at the
end of such a day, this small young hand feeling for her,
called her back from some despair where she had lived
these many months. She was mother again and she

171

looked at her child and coming clear at last from out her daze she cried, "Are your eyes worse, my child?"

And the girl answered, "I think I am as I ever was, except light seems to burn me more, and I do not see your faces clear as once I did, and now my brother grows so tall, I cannot tell if it be you or he who comes, unless I hear you speak."

Then the mother, leading this child of hers most tenderly, groaned to herself, "Where have I been these many days? Child, I will go tomorrow when dawn comes and buy some balm to make you well as I ever said I would!"

That night it seemed to all of them as though the mother had returned from some far place and was herself again. She put their bowls full of food upon the table and bestirred herself, her face pale and spent but tranquil and full of some wan peace. She looked at each child as though she had not seen him for a year or two. Now she looked at the little boy and she cried, "Son, tomorrow I will wash your coat. I had not seen how black it is and ragged. You are too pretty a lad to go so black as that and I your mother." And to the elder one she said, "You told me you had a finger cut and sore the other day. Let me see it." And when she washed his hand clean and put some oil upon the wound, she said, "How did you do it, son?"

And he opened his eyes surprised and said, "I told you,

mother, that I cut it when I made the sickle sharp upon the whetting stone and ready to reap the barley soon."

And she made haste to answer, "Aye, I remember now, you said so."

As for the children, they could not say how it was, but suddenly there seemed warmth about them and this warmth seemed to come from their mother and good cheer filled them and they began to talk and tell her this and that and the little lad said, "I have a penny that I gained today when we were tossing in the street to see who could gain it, and ever I gain the penny first I am so lucky."

And the mother looked on him avidly and saw how fair and sound a lad he was and while she wondered at herself because she had not seen it long ago, she answered him with hearty, sudden love, "Good lad to save the penny and not buy sweet stuff and waste it!" But at this the lad grew grave and said, troubled, "But only for today, mother, for tomorrow I had thought to buy the stuff and there is no need to save it for I can gain a penny every day or so," and he waited for her to refuse him, but she only answered mildly, "Well, and buy it, son, for the penny is your own."

Then the silent elder lad came forth with what he had to say, and he said, "My mother, I have a curious thing to tell you and it is this. Today when we were in the field, the landlord's agent and I, he said it was the last year he would come to this hamlet, for he is going out to try destiny in other parts. He said he was aweary of this walking over country roads and he was aweary of these common farmers and their wives, and it was the same thing season after season, and he was going to some city far from here."

This the mother heard and she paused to hear it, and she sat motionless and staring at the lad through the dim light of the flickering candle she had lit that night and set upon the table. Then when he was finished she waited for an instant and let the words sink in her heart. And they sank in like rain upon a spent and thirsty soil and she cried in a low warm voice, "Did he say so, my son?" and then as though it mattered nothing to her she added quickly, "But we must sleep and rest ourselves for tomorrow when the dawn comes I go to the city to buy the balm for your sister's eyes and make her well again."

And now her voice was full and peaceful, and when the dog came begging she fed him well and recklessly, and the beast ate happy and amazed, gulping all down in haste and sighing in content when he was full and fed.

That night she slept. They all slept and sleep covered them all, mother and children, deep and full of rest.

XII

THE next day came gray and still with unfinished rain of summer and the sky pressed low over the valley heavy with its burden of the rain, and the hills were hidden. But the mother rose early and made ready to take the girl to the town. She could not wait a day more to do what she could for this child of hers. She had waited all these many days and even let them stretch out into years, but now in her new motherhood, washed clean by tears, she could not be too tender or too quick for her own heart.

As for the young girl, she trembled with excitement while she combed her long hair and braided it freshly with a pink cord, and she put on a clean blue coat flowered with white, for she never in all her life had been away from this small hamlet, and as she made ready she said wistfully to them all, "I wish my eyes were clear today so I could see the strange sights in the town."

But the younger lad, hearing this, answered sharply and cleverly, "Yes, but if your eyes were clear you would not need to go."

So apt an answer was it that the young girl smiled as she ever did at some quick thing he said, but she an-

175

swered nothing, for she was not quick herself but slow and gentle in all she did, and when she had thought a while she said, "Even so, I had rather have my eyes clear and never see the town, perhaps. I think I would rather have my eyes clear."

But she said this so long after that the lad had forgotten what he said, being impatient in his temper and swift to change from this to that in play or bits of tasks he did, and indeed, he was more like his father than was any of the three.

But the mother did not listen to the children's talk. She made ready and she clothed herself. Once she stood hesitating by a drawer she opened and she took a little packet out and looked at it, opening the soft paper that enwrapped it, and it was the trinkets, and she thought, "Shall I keep them or shall I turn them into coin again?" And she doubted a while and now she thought, "True it is I can never wear them again, being held a widow, nor could I bear to wear them anyhow. But I could keep them for the girl's wedding." So she mused staring down at them in her hand. But suddenly remembering, her gorge rose against them and she longed to be free from them and from every memory and she said suddenly with resolve, "No, keep them I will not. And he might come home—my man might come home, and if he found me with strange trinkets he would not believe me if I told him I had bought them myself." So she thrust the

packet in her bosom and called to the girl they must set
forth.

They went along the country road and through the
hamlet before there was a stir, it was so early. The
mother strode freely, strong again as she had not been
for long, her head high and free against the misty air,
and she led her daughter by the hand, and the girl
struggled to move quickly, too. But she had not known
how little she could see. About the well known ways of
home her feet went easily and surely enough and she
did not know she went by feel and scent and not by
sight, but here the road was strange to her, now high,
now low, for the stones were sunken sometimes, and
often she would have fallen had it not been for her
mother's hand.

Then the mother seeing this was frightened and her
heart ran ahead to meet this fresh evil and she cried out
afraid, "I doubt I have brought you too late, poor child.
But you never told me that you could not see and I
thought it was but the water in your eyes that kept you
blinded."

And the girl half sobbing answered, "I thought I saw
well enough, too, my mother, and I think I do, only this
road is so up and down, and you go more quickly than I
am used to go."

Then the mother slowed her steps and said no more
and they went on, more slowly, save that when they
came near to that shop of medicine the mother made

haste again without knowing that she did, she was so eager. It was still early in the day and they were the first buyers and the medicine seller was but taking down the boards from his shop doors, and he did it slowly, stopping often to yawn and thrust his fingers into his long and uncombed hair and scratch his head. When he looked up and saw this countrywoman and the girl standing there before his counter he was amazed and he cried out, "What is it you want at such an early hour?"

Then the mother pointed to her child and she said, "Is there any balm that you have for such eyes as these?"

The man stared at the girl then and at her seared and red-rimmed eyes that she could scarcely open at all so red and seared they were, and he said, "How has she come by such eyes?"

The mother answered, "At first we thought it was the smoke made them so. My man is dead and I have a man's work to do on the land, and often has she fed the fire if I came home late. But these last years it seems more than this, for I have saved her the smoke, and there seems some heat that comes up in her of its own accord and burns her eyes. What fire it can be I do not know, being as she is the mildest maid, and never even out of temper."

Then the man shook his head, yawning widely again, and he said carelessly, "There are many who have eyes like these from some fire in them, various fires they be, and there is no balm to heal such fever. It will come up and up. Aye, and there is no healing."

Now these words fell like iron upon the two hearts that heard them and the mother said in a low swift voice, "But there may be—there must be some physician somewhere. Do you know of any good physician not too costly, since we be poor?"

But the man shook his tousled head languidly and went to fetch some drug he kept in a little box of wood, and he said as he went, "There is no skill to make her see, and this I know for I have seen a many such sore eyes, and every day people come here with such eyes and cry of inner fever. Aye, and even those foreign doctors have no true good way I hear, for though they cut the eyes open again and rub the inner part with magic stones and mutter runes and prayers, still the inner fires come up and burn the eyes again, and none can cut away that fire for it burns inside the seat of life. Yet here is a cooling powder that will cool a little while, though heal it cannot."

And he fetched a powder rolled in little grains like wheat and the color of a dark wheat, and he put them into a goose quill and sealed the other end with tallow and he said again, "Aye, she is blind, goodwife." And when he saw how the young girl's face looked at this news and how she was bewildered like a child is who has received a heavy unseen blow, he added, half kindly, too, "And what use to grieve? It is her destiny. In some other life she must have done an evil thing, looked on some forbidden sight, and so received this curse. Or else her father may have sinned, or even you, goodwife—who knows the heart? But however that may be the curse is here upon her and none can change what heaven wills." And again he yawned, his brief kindness done, and he took the pence the woman gave him and shuffled into some inner room.

As for the mother, she spoke back with brave anger and she said, "She is not blind! Whoever heard of sore eyes making people blind? My man's mother's eyes were sore from childhood, but she did not die blind!" And she went quickly before the man could make an answer, and she held the girl's hand hard to stay its trembling, and she went to a silversmith, not to that same one, and she took from her bosom that packet and she gave it to the bearded man who kept the shop and said, in a low voice, "Change me these into coin, for my man is dead and I cannot wear them more."

Then while the old man weighed out the trinkets to see what their worth was in coin, she waited and the young girl began to sob a little softly in her sleeve and then she said out from her sobs, "I do not believe I am truly blind, mother, for it seems to me I see something shining there on the scales, and if I were blind I could not see it, could I? What is that shining?"

Then the mother knew the girl was blind indeed, or good as blind, for the trinkets lay bright and plain not two feet from the girl's face, and she groaned in herself and she said, "You are right, too, child, and it is a bit of silver I had in a ring and I cannot wear now, and so I change it into coin we can use."

And in this new sorrow come upon her the woman gave no single thought to the trinkets when they were gone or thought of what they meant. No, she only thought of this, that with all their silvery shining her child could not see them, and the old man took them and hung them in his little case where he kept bracelets and rings and chains for children's necks and such pretty things, and she forgot all they had meant to her except, now, a shining thing her blind child could not see.

Yet was there one thing more to do, and she knew that she must do, if so be the child was to be truly blind. Holding the girl's hand she went along, shielding her from those who passed, for by now the streets were thronged and many came to buy and sell, farmers and gardeners setting their baskets of green and fresh vegetables along the sides of the streets, and fishermen setting out their tubs of fish there too. But the mother went until she came to a certain shop and she left the girl beside the door and went in alone, and when a clerk came forward to know what she would have, she pointed at a thing and said, "That," and it was the small brass gong and the little wooden hammer tied to it that the blind use when they walk to warn others they are blind. The clerk struck it once or twice to show its worth before he wrapped it, and hearing that sound the young girl lifted her head quickly and called, "Mother, there is a blind man here, for I hear a sound clear as a bell."

The clerk laughed loudly then, for well he saw the maid was blind, and he burst out, "There be none but—"

But the mother scowled at him so sourly that he left his words hanging as they were and gave the thing to her quickly and stood and stared like any fool at her while she went away, not knowing what to make of it.

They went home then and the young girl was contented to go home, for as the morning wore on the town grew full of noise and bustle and frightening sounds she was not used to hear and loud voices bawling in a bargain and rude thrusts against her from those she could not see, and she put her little foot here and there, feeling in her delicate way as she went, smiling unconsciously in her pain. But the mother grieved most bitterly in secret and she held hard in her other hand the thing she had bought, which is the sign of those who are blind.

Yet though she had this little gong, she could not give it to the girl. She could not take it that the girl's eyes were wholly sightless. She waited through the summer and they reaped the grain again, and it was measured to the new agent that the landlord sent, an old man this time, some poor cousin or distant kin, and autumn came, but still the mother could not give the girl the sign. No, there was a thing yet she must do, a prayer to make. For seeing daily her blind child, the mother remembered what the apothecary had said that day, "Some sin her parents did, perhaps—who knows the heart?"

She told herself that she would set forth to a temple that she knew—not to that wayside shrine nor ever to those gods whose faces she had covered—but to a temple far away, a whole ten miles and more, where she had heard there was a kind and potent goddess who heard women when they prayed bitterly. The mother told her two sons why she went and they were grave and awed to think what had befallen their sister. The elder said in his old man's way, "I have been long afraid there was a thing wrong with her." But the younger lad cried out astonished, "As for me, I never dreamed there was aught wrong with her eyes I am so used to her as she is!"

And the mother told the maid too and she said, "Daughter, I go to the temple to the south where there is that living goddess, and it is the selfsame one who gave the son to Li the Sixth's wife when she had gone barren all her life long and she was nearing the end of her time to bear, and her man grew impatient and would have taken a concubine he was so angry with her barrenness, and she went and prayed and there came that fine good son she has."

And the maid answered, "Well I remember it, mother, and she made two silken shoes for the goddess and gave

them when the boy was born. Aye, mother, go quickly,
for she is a true good goddess."

So the mother set forth alone, and all day she struggled
against the wind which blew unceasing through this
month, blowing down the cold with it as it came out of
the desert north, so that the leaves shriveled on the trees
and the wayside grass turned crisp and sere and all things
came to blight and death. But heavier than the wind,
more bitter, was the fear of the mother now and she
feared that her own sin had come upon the child. When
at last she came into the temple she did not see at all
how great and fine it was, its walls painted rosy red and
the gods gilded and many people coming to and fro for
worship. No, she went quickly in, searching out that one
goddess that she knew, and she bought a bit of incense
at the door where it was sold, and she said to the first
gray priest she saw, "Where is the living goddess?"

Then he, supposing her from her common looks to be
but one of those many women who came each day to
ask for sons, pointed with his pursed mouth to a dark
corner where a small old dingy goddess sat between two
lesser figures who attended her. There the mother went
and stood and waited while an old bent woman muttered her prayers for a son who could not move and had
lain these many years, she told the goddess, on his bed,
so stricken he could not even beget a son again, and the
old woman prayed and said, "If there be a sin in our
house for which we have not atoned, then tell me, lady

goddess, if this is why he lies there, and I will atone—I will atone!"

Then the old woman rose and coughing and sighing she went her way and the mother knelt and said her wish, too. But she could not forget what the old woman had said, and to the mother it seemed the goddess looked down harshly, and that the smooth golden face stared down fixed and unmoved by the sinful soul who prayed, whose sin was not atoned.

So the mother rose at last and sighed most heavily, not knowing what her prayer was worth, and she lit her incense and went away again. When she had walked the ten miles and come to her own door once more, cold and weary, she sank upon the stool and she said sadly when the children asked her how the goddess heard her prayer, "How do I know what heaven wills? I could but say my prayer and it must be as heaven wills and we can only wait and see how it will be."

But with all her secret heart she wished she had not sinned her sin. The more she wished the more she wondered how she could have done it, and all her gorge rose against that smooth-faced man and she loathed him for her sin's sake and because she could not now in any way undo what had been done. At that hour of deep loathing she was healed of all her heat and youth, and she was young no more. For her there was no man left in the world for man's own sake, and there were only these three her children, and one blind.

XIII

NOW the mother was no longer young. She was in her forty and third year, and when she counted on her fingers sometimes in the night how many years her children's father had been gone, she used the fingers of her two hands and two more over again, and even the years that she had let the hamlet think him dead were more than all the fingers on one hand.

Yet she walked straight and slight as ever, and no flesh grew on her frame. Others might begin to shrivel or grow fat as the cousin's wife did each year, and the old gossip, too, yet this woman stayed lean and strong as she had been when she was young. But her breasts grew small and dry, and in the strong sunlight where one saw her face full, there were lines about the eyes from working in the bright hard sunshine, and the skin was dark with the burning of the many years in the fields. She moved somewhat more slowly than she did, too, without the old lightness, for she had never been as she was before she tore that wild life out of her. When she was called for childbirth in the hamlet as she often was now, seeing she was widowed and counted as among the ones not young, she found it hard to move so quickly as she must sometimes, and once or twice a young mother caught the child herself, and once she even let a newborn babe fall to the brick floor and bruise its head, and it was a boy, too, but still no harm was done in the end most luckily, for the lad grew up sturdy and with all his senses in him.

As her children grew, to them their mother seemed old. The eldest was forever urging her to rest herself and not to heave so at the hard great clods when the land was ploughed but let him do it, for he did it easily now in the strength of his young manhood, and he strove to have her do the lesser lighter things, and nothing pleased him better than to see her sit quietly upon her stool in the shade on a summer's day sewing, and let him go to the land alone.

Yet the truth was she was not after all as old as her son would have her. She ever loved the field work better than any and she loved to work there on the land and then come home, her body wet with her clean sweat and the wind blowing cool on that wetness, and her flesh weary but sweetly so. Her eyes were used to fields and hills and great things, and they did not narrow easily to small fine things like needles.

Indeed, in that house they sorely missed a woman young and with sound eyes, for they all knew now the girl's eyes were blind. She knew, too, poor maid; ever since that day when she had gone to town with her

THE MOTHER

mother she knew it secretly, even as her mother did, and neither had any great faith in the goddess, somehow, the mother from what she feared of that old sin of hers, and the maid because her blindness seemed to her a destiny.

One day the mother cried, "Have you used that stuff all gone from the goose quill?" and the girl answered quietly from the doorstep where she sat, for there was this one good she had, the light hurt her no more because she could not see it, and she said, "I have used it to the end long since."

And the mother said again, "I must buy you more—why did you not say it sooner?"

But the young girl shook her head, and the mother's heart stopped to see her look, and then these words came wildly from those gentle lips, "Oh, mother, I am blind—well I know I am blind! I cannot see your face at all now, and if I went out from our own dooryard across the threshing-floor, I could not see the way to go. Do you not see I never go away from the house now, not even to the field?" And she fell to weeping, wincing and biting her lips, for it was still painful to her to weep, and she would not unless she could not help herself.

The mother answered nothing. What was there to answer to her blind child? . . . But after a while she rose and went into the room and from the drawer where once the trinkets lay she fetched out the little gong she bought and she said to the girl, going to her, "Child, I bought this thing against the day—" She could not

189

finish but she pressed the thing into the girl's hand and the girl took it, feeling quickly what it was, and she held it fast and said in her plaintive way, quiet again, "Yes, I need it, mother."

When the elder son came home that evening his mother bade him cut a staff from some hard tree and smooth it to his sister's hand, so that with her little sounding signal in one hand and in the other the staff she might move about more freely and with something less of fear, as the blind do, and so if any harm came to her, or one pushed against her carelessly or knocked her so she fell, the mother would not be blamed because she had set the sign of blindness plain upon the maid for all to see.

Thereafter the young girl carried with her when she went outside the door at all these two things, her staff and her small gong, and she learned to tinkle the gong softly and clearly and she moved in a quiet sure way, a pretty maid enough, her face small and plaintive and on it that still look that blindness sets upon a face.

Yet this blind maid was wonderfully clever, too, in her own way about the house. There she needed no sign or staff, and she could wash the rice and cook it, save that her mother would not let her light the fire any more, but she could sweep the room and the threshing-floor, and she could draw water from the pool, and search for eggs if the fowls laid them in some usual place, and she knew by scent and sound where the beasts were and how to set their food before them, and almost everything she could do, except to sew and work in the fields, and for labor in the fields she was not strong enough, for her suffering from babyhood had seemed to stunt her and hold back her growth.

Seeing the young girl move thus about the house the mother's heart would melt within her and she suffered for what fate might befall this young thing when she must wed her somewhere. For wed she must be somehow, lest after the mother died there be not one to care for the maid nor one to whom she truly could belong, since a woman belongs first to the husband's house and not to that house where she was born. Often and often the mother thought of this and she wondered who would have a maid who was blind, and if none would have her then what would happen to her in the end. If ever she spoke this matter out the elder lad would answer, "I will care for her, mother, as long as she will do her share," and this would comfort the mother somewhat and yet she knew a man cannot be fully known until it is seen what his wife is, and she would think to herself, "I must find him such a wife as will take good heed of my blind maid and be kind to her. When I go looking for his wife I must find one who will take heed of two, her husband and his sister."

It was time, too, the mother found a wife for this elder son of hers. Nineteen years old he had got to be and almost without her knowing it. Yet he had never asked her for a wife nor shown her his need of one. Ever he had been the best and mildest son a mother could have, working hard and never asking anything and if he went to the teashop sometimes or rarely on a holiday in town, although that he never did unless he had some business to put with it, he never took share in any ribaldry, nor even in a game of chance except to watch it from afar, and he was always silent where his elders were.

A very perfect son he was and with but one fault left now that he had passed the little faults of childhood and it was that he would not spare his younger brother. No, it was the strangest thing, but this elder son of hers, who was so even and gentle with all the world and even with the beasts, so silent he would scarcely say what color he would have the next new coat his mother bought him, when he was brother he was hard upon the younger lad and railed against the boy if he grew slack and played, and he held the boy bitterly to every sort of labor on the land. The house was full of quarreling, the younger lad noisy and full of angry words, and the elder brother holding himself silent until he could bear no more and then he fell upon his brother with whatever he had by him or with his bare hands and he beat the boy until he ran blubbering and dodging in and out among the trees and seeking refuge in his cousin's house. And truly it came to such a pass as this, that the whole hamlet blamed the elder brother for his hardness and ran to save the younger lad, and so encouraged, the lad grew bold and ran away from work and lived mostly at his cousin's house, lost there among the many lads and maids who grew there as they would, and he came home freely only when he saw his brother gone to work.

But sometimes the elder brother grew so bitter in his heart he came home out of time and found his younger brother and then he caught the lad's head beneath his arm and cuffed him until the mother would come running and she cried, "Now let be—let be—shame on you, son, to strike your little brother so, and frighten your sister!"

But the young man answered bitterly, "Shall I not chastise him, being older brother to him and his father gone? He is an idle lazy lout, gaming already every time he can, and well you know it, mother, but you have ever loved him best!"

It was true the mother did love this youngest son the best, and he moved her heart as neither of the others did. The eldest son grew man so soon, it seemed to her, and silent and with naught to say to anyone, and she did not know this was because he was so often weary and that she thought him surly when he was only very weary. As for the girl, the mother loved her well but always with pain, for there the blind eyes were always for a reproach and she never could forget that the goddess had not heard her prayer nor had the mother ever heart to pray again, fearing now that it was her own sin come down in some way worse than she could bear because it fell upon her child. So it was that while her heart was ever soft with pity still the maid was never any joy to her. Even when the maid came loving and near and smiling and sat to listen to her mother's voice, the mother rose with some excuse and busied herself somehow, because she could not bear to see those closed and empty eyes.

Only this youngest son was sound and whole and merry and oftentimes he seemed his father over again, and more and more the mother loved him, and all the love she ever had for the man now turned itself upon this son. She loved him and often stood between him and the elder brother so that when the young man seized the boy she rushed between them and caught the blows and forced her son to cease for shame because he might strike his mother, and then the lad would slip away.

It came to be that after a while the lad slipped often thus away and from his hiding in his cousin's house he went to wandering here and there and even to the town and he would be gone perhaps a day or two, and then he would run back to his cousin's house and come out as if he had been there all the time, his eyes upon his elder brother's mood that day. And if he did not come, the mother would wait until the elder son was gone and she went to the cousin's house and coaxed him home with some dainty she had made. But she half feared her elder son too these days and sometimes she would start with

him to the field or leave soon and come and give the lad
his meal first before his brother came, and he picked the
best from every dish and she let him, for she loved him
so well. She loved him for his merry words and ways and
for his smooth round face and for the same supple, lis-
some body that his father had. The elder lad went bent
already with his labor, his hand hard and slow, but this
lad was quick and brown and smooth-skinned everywhere and light upon his feet as a young male cat, and
the mother loved him.

And the slow elder son felt this warm love his mother
had for his brother, and he brooded on it. Every day of
labor he had done, and all the labor that he spared her
he remembered now and it seemed to him his mother
was the cruelest soul that ever lived and she never recked
it anything that he had striven from childhood for her
sake. So the bitterness gathered slow and deep within his
heart, and he hated his brother.

XIV

NOW all this hatred gathered in the elder son and even the mother did not know how deep it was until a certain day when out it came, bursting forth like a river dammed behind a dyke and swollen with waters from small secret sources that men do not know, so that when it breaks they are astonished because none knew how it had been with that river all the days when it had seemed the same.

It was at the time of the rice harvest at the end of a summer when all must labor hard and heavily upon the land from dawn to dark, and so everyone must labor who is not rich enough to hire it done for him. Now the young lad had labored that day, too, although he usually thought of some distant thing he had to do elsewhere. But this time the mother had coaxed him to it and she had said to him secretly, smoothing his bony lad's hand while she talked, "Work well for these few days, my son, while the harvest lasts, and show your brother how well you can do, and if you will work well and please him then I will buy you something pretty when the work is done, something that you want most."

So the lad promised he would, pouting his red lips

and feeling himself hard used, and he worked well enough, although not too well, yet well enough to save his skin when his brother's eye fell on him.

But that day when a rain threatened before the sheaves were in, they all worked beyond the usual hour and the mother worked until she was spent, for she had never been so tireless as she was before she ate the bitter herbs to save her honor that dark night. Then she sighed and straightened her aching back and said, "My son, I will go home and see the food is heated for you when you come, for I am spent and sore."

"Go home, then," said the elder son a little roughly, yet not meaning to be so, for he never urged his mother to do more than she would. So she went then, and left the brothers alone, for the hour grew too late even for the gleaners who had followed them by day.

Scarcely had she set the food to boiling when the maid cried out from where she sat upon the threshold that she heard her little brother weeping, and when the mother ran out of the kitchen it was so and she ran to the harvest field and there upon the reaped grain the elder son was beating the younger one most mercilessly with the handle of his scythe, and the younger one was howling and striking back with his two fists and struggling to loose himself from his brother's hard grasp about his neck. But the elder brother held him fast and beat him with the dull end of the handle. Then the mother ran with all her strength and clung to the angry elder son and begged of him, "Oh, my son, a little lad he is yet—Oh, son. Oh, son!"

And as she clung like this the younger slipped out from the elder's hand and ran swift as a young hare across the field and disappeared into the dusk. There were these two left, the mother and her bitter elder son. Then she faltered, "He is such a child yet, son, only fourteen and with his mind still on play."

But the young man replied, "Was I child at fourteen? Did I play at harvest time when I was fourteen and needed I to have you bribe me with a ring and a new robe and this and that I had not earned?"

Then she knew the silly younger lad had boasted of what he would have and she stood speechless, caught in her fault, staring at her son and silent, and he went on and cried, his bitterness bursting from him, "Yes, you keep the money, and I give you all we earn. I never take a penny for my own, not even to smoke a little pipe of any kind or take a bowl of wine or buy myself anything a young man might have and count it but his due. Yet you must promise him all I never had! And for what? To do the labor that he ought to do for nothing and to pay for what he eats and wears!"

"I did not promise rings and robes," she said in a low and troubled voice, half afraid of this angry son of hers who was so grave and quiet on other days that she did not know him now.

"You did!" he said most passionately. "Or if not that,

then worse, for he said he was to have what he wanted when the harvest money was in and taxes paid. He said you promised!"

"I meant some small toy or other, costing but a penny or so," she answered, shamed before this good son of hers. And then plucking up her courage—for was he not her son still?—she added, "And if I did promise a little toy it was but to save him from your angers on him always, whatever he may do, so that you keep him down with all your cruel looks and words—and now blows!"

But he would say no more. He fell to the sheaves again and worked as though some demon had him, he worked so hard and fast. The mother stood looking at him, not knowing what to do, feeling he was hard, too, with her little son, and yet knowing somehow she was wrong. Then as she looked she saw the young man was very near to tears, so that he set his jaws hard to keep back a sob, and when she saw this sign of feeling in him, such as she had never seen in him who always seemed so usual and content and without any desire, her heart grew soft as ever it did when she had harmed a child of hers, although he did not know it, and she softened to him more than she had ever done before and she cried quickly, "Son, I am wrong, I know. I have not done well enough for you of late. I have not seen how you have grown into a man. But man you are, and now I see it, and you shall take the man's place in our house and you shall have the money and the chief place in name as well as in the labor you have always done. Yes, I see you are a man now, and I will do straightway what I have put off too long. I will find a wife for you and it will be your turn now and hers. I have not seen it, but now I see it well."

So she made amends. He muttered something then that she could not hear and turned his back and said no more but worked on. But she felt eased by her amends and went back crying briskly, "Well, and all the rice will be burned, I swear—" and this she said to cover up the feeling of the moment and make it usual.

But when she was home again she busied herself here and there forgetting all her weariness, and when the maid asked, "Mother, what was wrong?" she answered quickly, "Nothing much amiss, child, except your younger brother would not do his share, or so his brother said. But brothers always quarrel, I think," and she ran and made an extra dish from some radishes she pulled, and sliced them and poured vinegar upon them and sesame oil and soy sauce, such as she knew her son loved. And as she worked she pondered her amends and it seemed true to her her son should wed and she blamed herself because she had leaned on him as on a man, and yet he had not man's reward, and she set her mind to do all that she had said she would.

Her elder son came in at last and later than usual so that it was wholly dark and she could not see his face until he came within the light of the candle she had lit and set ready on the table. She looked at him closely then, without his seeing her, and she saw he was himself again and pleased with what she had said and all his anger gone. And seeing this peace upon her elder son she called to the younger one who hung about the door, not daring to come in until he knew his brother's temper, and yet driven by hunger, too, and she called out, "Come in, little son!"

And he came in, his eyes upon his brother. But the elder paid no heed to him, his anger gone for this time, and the mother was well content and knew she had decided well and so she moved to carry out her promise to the end.

And as she ever did in any little trouble, she went to the cousin and to the cousin's wife, for she herself knew no maid, since none in that hamlet could be chosen, seeing all were kin by blood and marriage and had the same surname, nor did she know any maid in town, for there she had dealings only with such small shops as bought the little she had to sell. She went at an hour in evening, for the year was yet warm although early autumn was near, and they sat and talked while the cousin's wife suckled her last child. The mother made known her want at last and said, "Then do you know any maid, my sister, in that village where you lived before you were wed? A maid like yourself I would like very well, easy tempered and quick to bear and good enough at labor. The house I can tend myself yet for many a year, and if she be not so good in the house I can endure it."

The good cousin's wife laughed at this loudly and looked at her man and cried, "I do not know if he would say your son would count it curse or blessing to have one like me."

Then the man looked up in his slow way, a bit of rice stalk in his mouth which he had sat chewing as he listened, and he answered thoughtfully, "Oh, aye—good enough—" and his wife laughed again to hear his luke-warmness and then she said, "Well, and I can go there and see, sister, and there are two hundred families or so in that village, a market-town it is, and doubtless one maid among so many ready to be wed."

So they talked on of it and the mother said plainly there must not be too great a cost, and she said, "I know very well I cannot hope for one of the very best in every way, since I am poor and my son has no great lot of land and we must rent more than we own."

But the man spoke up and said to this, "Well, but you do own some land, and it is something nowadays when many have nothing at all, and I had liefer wed a maid of mine to a man who has some land and little silver than to one who has much silver and no firm land to stand on. A good man and good land—that would be sound promise for any maid if she were mine." And when his wife said, "Well, then, children's father, if you will let me go,

I can go to that town a day or two, and look about,"
then he said in his spare way, "Oh, aye, I will—the
maids are old enough to free you now and then."

So soon thereafter the cousin's wife dressed herself
clean and took the babe and a child or two among the
little ones to show her father's family and she took an
elder two or so to help her with the little ones, and hired
a wheelbarrow to put them all upon and she rode her
husband's gray ass he did not need these days now that
the harvest was over and he could use his ox to tread
the grain. They set forth thus and were gone three days
and more. And when she was come back she was right
full of all the maids that she had seen and she said to
the mother, who ran to hear her when the news came
she had returned,

"Maids there be a plenty in that village for we never
kill them there as they do in some towns when babes
are girls, and they are allowed to grow however many a
mother has, and so the village is full of them. I saw a
dozen that I knew myself, sister, all well grown and full
of flesh and color, and any would have done for any son
I have. But still only one was needed and I narrowed
my two eyes and looked at this one and that one, and
chose out three, and out of the three I looked again and
saw one had a cough and a bubbly nose, and one was
with some soreness of the eyes, and the third was best.
She is a sharp and clever maid, I swear, very careful in
all she says and does, and they say she is the quickest

seamstress in the town. She makes her own clothes and clothes for all her father's house and some for others and turns a bit of silver in. A little old she is, perhaps, for your lad, because once she was betrothed, and the man died out of time, or she would be wed by now. But this is not ill, either, for the father is eager to wed her somehow and will not ask much for her. She is not so pretty perhaps as the others—her face a little yellow from sewing overmuch, but she is clean-eyed."

Then the mother answered quickly, "We have sore eyes enough in our house, I swear, and my eyes are not what they were either, and we need someone who sews and likes it. Settle it then, my sister, with this one, and if she is not above five years older than my son, it is well enough."

So was it done, and the days of the month and the years in which the two were born and the hours of their birth were compared upon a geomancer's table in the town, and they were all favorable. The young man was born under the sign of horse, and the maid under the sign of cat, which do not devour each other, and thus was harmony foretold in the marriage. All things being right by destiny, therefore, the gifts that must be given were given.

Now out of her little hidden store the mother brought forth bits of silver and odd copper coins and she bought good cotton stuffs and made two garments for the maid, herself. And as the custom was in those parts she wished a lucky woman to cut the garments, some woman whose life was whole with man and sons. What woman then was more lucky in the hamlet than the cousin's wife? The mother took the good stuff to her and said, "Set your hand here, my sister, so that your luck may fall upon my son's wife."

And so the cousin's wife did, and she cut the garments wide and full across the belly so that when the maid conceived they could be worn with ease and not laid aside to waste.

And the mother put forth more silver and hired the red marriage chair and the bead crown and the earrings of false pearls and all that was needful for the day, and especially the trousers of red which every bride must wear in those parts. So was the marriage day set and it drew on, and dawned at last, a clear cold day in the winter of that year.

Now was it a strange day for this mother when she must welcome to her house a new and younger woman, so long had she been master there as well as mistress. When she was dressed in her best and stood waiting at her door, when she saw the red bridal chair come near with its burden of the bride within, it seemed suddenly but a little while ago when she herself had come in that same chair, and the old woman dead stood where she stood today and her own man where her son stood. Rarely did she think these days of that man of hers, and truly did he seem dead to her, but the strangest longing fell on her for him while she stood waiting. It was not the longing of the flesh; no, that was dead and gone now. It was some other longing, the longing for some completeness of her own age, for she felt alone.

She looked at her son newly, no longer only son to her, but husband to another now, and there he stood, very still, his head hung down, stiff in the new black robe she had made for him, and shoes upon his feet most often bare. He seemed unmoved, or so she thought until she saw his hanging hands trembling against the black of his robe. She sighed again then, and again she thought of her own man and how she had peeped out at him from behind the curtains of her chair and how her heart leaped to see how fair he was and how good a man to look on in every way. Yes, he had been prettier far than this son of hers was today, and she thought to herself now that he was the prettiest man she had ever seen.

But before she had time to grieve more than in this dim way the first of the procession came, the small wedding fruits, the cock she had sent to the bride's house and that according to custom they sent back and with it a hen they mated to it, and after these few things, the chair was fetched and set down there before the door and the cousin's wife and the gossip and the other elder women of the hamlet took the bride's hand and tried to pull her forth. And she was proper and reluctant and came at last but most unwillingly, and when she did come she made her eyes downcast and did not look up once. Then the mother withdrew into her cousin's house, as was the custom too in those parts where it was said a son's wife must not see too easily her husband's mother, lest she do not fear her thereafter, and all that day the mother stayed in the cousin's house.

But still she stayed near the door to hear what people said of this new wife, and she heard some cry, "A very good and earnest-looking maid," and some said, "They say she sews well, and if it is true she made those shoes she wears, she has ten good fingers, I swear!" And some among the women went up and fingered the red wedding robes and lifted the coat to see the inner ones, and all were well and neatly made, and the buttons hard and nicely turned of twisted cloth, and they ran and told the mother all, "A decent, able maid, goodwife, and with a proper look." But some among the men spoke coarsely and one said, "Too thin and yellow for my taste, I swear!" and another called out, "Aye, but a few months will mend the thinness, brother—naught like a man to make a maid swell!"

And in all this merry, ribald talk the maid moved demurely to her new home and so was wed.

Now must the mother leave the bed where she had slept these many years, and when the daughter-in-law came to make the bed for the mother that night, for so it was done in those parts, she made the pallet where the old dead woman once had slept behind the curtains, and

later the elder son; and the blind girl had a pallet of her own beside it, and the younger lad slept in the kitchen if he slept at home. Yes, upon the true bed the elder son slept now with his new wife.

It was not easy either for the mother to give up to this new pair that place which had been hers and her man's, and it made her seem old to herself at night to lie on the old woman's pallet. Through the day she could be usual, busy everywhere, commanding all, her tongue quick to correct and command, but at night she was old. Oftentimes she woke and it seemed to her it could not be she who lay there and the other pair upon the bed, and she thought to herself amazed, "Now I suppose that old soul who was mother when I came to this house felt as I do now, when I came a bride and pushed her from her bed and lay there with her son in my turn. And now another lies with my son."

It seemed so strange, so endless, this turning of some hidden wheel, this passing on of link caught onto link in some never ending chain that she was dazed with thinking of it even dimly, since she was not one to think into the meanings of what passed before her, but only taking all that came for what it was. But she was lessened in her own eyes from that day on. Even though she was in name the oldest and the first and mistress over all, she was not first in her own eyes.

And she watched this son's wife. She was dutiful and day after day she made her bow before her husband's mother, until the mother grew weary and shouted at her, "Enough!" But the mother could not find any fault in her. Then was this very faultlessness a fault and the mother muttered, "Well, and doubtless she has some secret inner fault I do not see at once."

For the son's wife did not, as some maids do, set forth all that she was at once. She was diligent and she was smooth and quick at work and when the work was done she sat and sewed on something for her husband but all she did was done in her own careful way.

Now there are not two women in this world who do the same task alike, and this the mother had not known, thinking all did as she did. But no, this son's wife had her own way of doing all. When she cooked the rice she put too much water in, or so the mother thought, and the rice came out softer than the mother was used or liked to have it. And she told the son's wife so, but that one shut her pale lips smoothly and said, "But so I ever do it." And she would not change.

Thus it was with everything. This and that about the house she changed to her own liking, not quickly nor in any temper, but in a small, careful, gradual way, so that it gave the mother no handle to lay her anger on. There was another thing. The young wife did not like the smell of beasts at night, and made complaint, but not to the older woman, only to the man, until he set to work that same winter to add a room to the house where they could move the bed in and sleep alone. And the older woman looked on astonished at such new ways.

At first she said to the blind maid that she would not be angry with the son's wife. And indeed it was not easy to be angry quickly, for the young wife did well and worked carefully, so that it was hard to say "this is wrong" or "you did not do that well." But there were things the mother hated somehow, though most she loathed the softened rice and of it she grumbled often and at last aloud, "I never do feel full and fed with such soft stuff. There is naught to set my teeth down on—this watery stuff, it passes my belly like a wind and does not lie like firm good food." And when she saw her son's wife pay no heed to this she went secretly to her son one day where he worked in the field and there she said, "Son, why do you not bid her cook the rice more dry and hard? I thought you used to like it so."

The son stopped his labor then and stayed himself a moment on his hoe and said in his calm way, "I like it as she does it very well."

Then the mother felt her anger rise and she said, "You did not use to like it so and it means you have joined yourself to her instead of me. It is shameful that you like her so and go against your mother."

Then the red came flooding into the young man's face and he said simply, "Aye, I like her well enough," and fell to his hoe again.

From that day on the mother knew the two were

masters in the house. The eldest son was not less kind than usual and he did his work well and took the money into his own hand. It was true he did not spend it, nor did his wife, for the two were a saving pair, but they were man and wife and this their house and land, and to them the mother was but the old woman in the house. It was true that if she spoke of field or seed and of all the labor that she knew so well because it had been hers, they let her speak, but yet when she had finished it was as though she had not spoken, and they made their plans and carried all on as they liked. It seemed to her she was nothing any more, her wisdom less than nothing in the house that had been hers.

Very bitter was it for anyone to bear and when the new room was made and the pair moved into it, the mother muttered to the blind girl who slept beside her, "I never saw such finicking as this, as though the honest smell of beasts was poison! I do swear they made that room so they could be away from us and talk their plans we cannot hear. They never tell me anything. It is not the beasts—it is that your brother loves her shamefully. Yes, they care nothing for you or for your little brother, nor even for me, I know." And when the girl did not answer she said, "Do you not think so, too, my maid? Am I not right?"

Then the maid hesitated and she said after a while out of the darkness, "Mother, it is true I have something to say I would say and yet I would not, lest it grieve you."

Then the mother cried out, "Say on, child. I am used to grief, I think."

And then the maid asked in a small sad voice, "Mother, what will you do with me, blind as I am?"

Now all this time the mother had not thought otherwise than that this maid would live on here with her a while at least and she said in surprise, "What do you mean, my maid?"

And the maid said, "I do not mean my brother's wife is not kind—she is not cruel, mother. But I think she does not dream you will not wed me soon. I heard her ask my little brother but the other day where I was betrothed, and when he said I was not she said surprised, 'A great maid to be without a mother-in-law still.' "

"But you are blind, child," said the mother, "and it is not so easy to wed a blind maid."

"I know it," said the maid gently. And after a while she spoke again, and this time as though her mouth were very dry and as though her breath came hot. "But you know there are many things I can do, mother, and there may be some very poor man, a widower, perhaps, or some such poor man who would be glad of the little I could do if he need pay nothing for me, and then would I be in my own house and there would be someone if you were gone whom I could care for. Mother, I do not think my sister wants me."

But the mother answered violently, "Child, I will not have you go to mend some man's house like that! We are poor, I know, but you can be fed. Widowers are often the hardest and lustiest husbands, child. So go to sleep and think no more of this. Hearty I am yet and likely to live a long full time yet, and your brother was never cruel to you, even as a child."

"He was not wed then, mother," said the girl, sighing. But she stayed silent then and seemed to sleep.

But the mother could not sleep a while, although on usual nights she slept deep and sound. She lay there thinking hard, and taking up the days past, one by one, to see if what the girl had said was true, and though she could not think of any single thing, it seemed to her the son's wife was not warm. No, she was not very warm to the younger lad either, and at least not warm to this blind sister in her husband's house, and here was new bitterness for the mother to bear.

XV

EVERY day the mother watched to see if what the girl had said was true, and it was true. The young wife was not rude, and her words came from her smoothly and with seeming careful courtesy always. But she put upon the maid a hundred little pricks. She gave the blind maid less than her full bowl of food, or so it seemed in the mother's eyes, and if there were some dainty on the table she did not give her any, and the blind maid, not seeing, did not know it was there. And indeed they would all have let it pass, not heeding in their own hunger, had not the mother's eyes been sharpened, and she cried out, "Daughter, do you not like this dish of pig's lungs we have cooked in soup today?"

And when the maid answered gently in surprise, "I did not know we had it, mother, and I like it very well," then the mother would reach over and with her own spoon dip the meat and soup into the maid's bowl, and be sure the son's wife saw the mother do it, and she answered smoothly and courteously, scarcely moving her pale lips that with all their paleness were too thick, too, and she said, "I beg your pardon, sister—I did not see you had none." But the mother knew she lied.

And sometimes when the son's wife sewed shoes for the maid, and it was her duty to make shoes for them all, she put no time on the maid's shoes beyond what she must, and she made the soles thin and spared herself the labor of a flower upon the front, and when the mother saw it she cried, "What—shall my maid not have a little flower such as you have on all your shoes?"

Then the son's wife opened her little, dark, unshining eyes and said, "I will make them if you say, mother, only I thought since she was blind and could not see a color anyhow—and I have so many to make shoes for, and the younger lad wearing out a pair each month or two with all his running into town to play—"

As for the blind maid who sat there on the threshold in the sun, when she heard this and heard the complaint her sister made against the younger brother, she cried out in mild haste, "Mother, indeed I do not care for the flower, and my sister is right. What are flowers to the blind?"

So it seemed no quarrel and all the many small things seemed no quarrel. Yet one day the eldest son came to his mother, when she went around the house alone to pour some waste into the pig's hole, and he said, "Mother, I have a thing to say to you, and it is not that I would urge my sister out of the house or grudge her anything. But a man must think of his own, and she is young, mother, and all her life is ahead of her, and shall I feed her all her life? I have not heard it so in any other house, that a man must feed his sister, unless it were some rich house where food is never missed. A man's duty it is to feed his parents, his wife and his children. But there she is, young and like to live as long as I do, and it will be an ill thing for her, too, if she is not wed. Better for all women to be wed."

Then the mother looked at her son, her face set in anger against him, and she said, accusing him, "That wife of yours has put this thought into you, my son. You lie there with her alone in that room and there you talk, the two of you, and she poisons you against your own blood with all she says to you in the night. And you—you are like all men—soft as mud in a ditch when you lie in bed with a woman."

She turned away most bitterly, and she poured the stuff out for the pig and stood and watched it put its snout in and gobble, but she did not really see it, although commonly it was a thing to give her pleasure to see a beast feed heartily. No, she said on in sadness, "And what sort of man will have your sister? Who can we hope will have her save some man too poor for kindness, or a man whose wife is gone and he left and too poor to wed a sound woman again?"

Then the son said hastily, "I think of her, too. I do think of her and I think it is better for her to have a man of her own, even though she cannot have so good a one as though she were whole."

217

"This is your wife who speaks, my son," the mother said more sadly still.

But the man made answer in his stubborn way, "We are of one heart on this," and when his mother said, "On everything, I fear," he said no more but went to his fields, silent but unchanged.

Nevertheless the mother wilfully would not for long do anything to wed the maid. She told herself and told the maid and told her younger son and her cousin's wife and any who would listen to her that she was not so old yet she could not have her own way and not so old she had no place in the house and not so old she could be bid like any child to do this or that or what she did not wish to do. She set herself against her son and son's wife in this and herself she guarded the maid well and saw that nothing was done amiss to her nor that she was deprived of anything the others had.

But as the son's wife grew more accustomed she grew more plain in speech and more complaining and courtesy dropped from her. She often said now where others heard her or when the women sat together about some door in the sun and sewed in company or had some gathering such as women love, then she said, "What I shall do when children come I do not know, seeing how I have to sew for all these in the house now. My mother grows old and I know it is my duty to do for her and be her eyes and hands and feet and all she needs. I have been taught so, and so I do and I hope I am always careful of my duty. But here this hungry second lad is and he does nothing, and here worse than he, for some day he must wed and his wife will work to feed and clothe him, here is this blind maid not wed and I do wonder if she is to be my care her whole life long, for her mother will not wed her."

Such words as these she said and others like them and those who heard stared at the blind maid if she were by so that she even felt their gaze and hung her head ashamed to live as such a burden. And sometimes this one spoke or that one and said, "Well and there are many blind and some families teach their blind to tell fortunes or some such thing and earn a penny now and then. Yes, the blind often have an inward seeing eye and they can see things we cannot and their blindness is even a power to them so that other people fear them for it. This maid might be taught to soothsay or some such thing."

And others said, "But there are poor houses, too, where they have a son and no money to wed him with and they will take a fool or a blind maid or one halt or dumb and count her better than none if they can get her for nothing for their son."

Then the son's wife said discontentedly, "I wish I knew some such one, and if you hear of any, neighbors, I would take it for a kindness if you would tell me so." And being kind they promised the young wife, and they agreed that truly it was hard when money was so scarce and times so poor that she must feed this extra mouth that properly belonged elsewhere.

One day the gossip who was a widow came to the mother and she said, "Goodwife, if you would like to wed that blind maid of yours, I know a family in the hills to the north and they have a son seventeen or so now. They came in famine times from a northern province and they settled on some wild public land not in our village at the mountain's foot, but up a little higher, and after a while a brother came, and there they live. The land is poor and they are poor, but so be you poor, too, goodwife, and your maid blind, and if you will only pay my going I will go and see to it for you. The truth is I have been minded for this long time to go home and see my own father's house, but I am loath to ask my husband's brother for the bit to do it with. A very hard thing is it to be widow in another's house."

At first the mother would not listen and she said loudly, "I can tend my own blind maid, goodwife!"

This afterwards she told her cousin's wife and the cousin too, but the cousin looked grave a while and he said at last, "So could you tend her if you lived forever, sister, but when you are dead, and we dead too, perhaps, or very old and not masters any more before our children save in name, then who will tend her? And what if bad years come and parents must think first of their own children, and you gone?"

Then the mother was silent.

But soon she saw the truth that she could not live forever, at any time her life might end, the sooner, too, perhaps, because she had never had her own old vigor since that secret night.

In the summer of that year a flux came out of the air and laid its hold upon her. Ever she had loved to eat and eat heartily and all she wanted of what there was. But that summer came more than usually hot and there was a mighty pest of flies, so many everywhere that the winds blew them in the food and flies were mingled whether one would have it so or not, and the mother cried out at last to let them be, for there was no use in killing them and it was but a waste of time so many more came after. It was a summer, too, of great watermelons that when they were split showed darkly red or clear and yellow as their sort was, and never had there been a better year for melons than was that.

Now well the mother loved this fruit, and she ate heartily of all such as could not be sold or such as grew too ripe suddenly beneath the sun, and she ate on and on and when she was filled, she ate yet more to keep the things from being wasted. Whether it was the many melons or whether some wicked wind caught her or whether someone laid a curse upon her, although she did not know of one who really hated her unless it were that little goddess who had guessed her sin, or what it was she did not know. But the flux came on her and it dragged her very inwards out and she lay ill for days, purged and retching up so much as a mouthful of tea she swallowed to stay herself if she could.

In these days when she was so racked and weak the son's wife did all well and everything she knew to do for her husband's mother's sake, nor was she lacking in any small duty. The blind maid strove to do her poor best too for her mother, but she was slow and could not see a need in time, and often the son's wife pushed the maid aside and said, "Do you sit down somewhere, good sister, and out of my way, for I swear you are the most help so!"

Even against her will then did the mother come to lean, in all her weakness, on this quick and careful younger woman, and she was too weak to defend her blind maid, and the younger son these days came but sometimes to see how she did and went away again somewhere because his mother was too weak to say a word for him against his brother. In such weakness it was a strength to the mother to feel the young wife deft and careful about her bed. When at last the flux passed out of her and to some other person destined for it, and the mother rose at last, she leaned hard upon her son's wife, though she did not love her either, but only needed her.

It took the mother very long to come somewhat to herself again, and she was never wholly sound again. She could not eat the rough cabbages she loved, nor any sort of melon nor the peanuts she had liked to chew raw from the ground when they were dug, and ever after this she had to think what she ate, to see how it suited itself to her inwards, and if she grew impatient with such finicking and cried out that she would eat what she would and liked and her belly must bear it, why, then the flux came back again. Or even if she worked too hard or sat in any small cold wind that evil illness waited for her and made her helpless for a while again.

Then in her helplessness she saw the blind maid must be wed into some house of her own, for it was true she was not welcome here. When the mother was too weak to cry against it, she saw the maid was ill at ease there and felt herself unwanted, and one day the maid came herself at a moment when her mother was alone and she said, "Mother, I cannot stay here in my brother's house. Oh, mother, I think I would sooner be wed anywhere so that I could be somewhere I was wanted!"

Then the mother said no more against it. She comforted her daughter with a word or two and one day in the winter of that year when she felt stronger than she had, for ever after she was better in the cold than in the heat, she went and sought the gossip out. There the old gossip sat in her doorway, stitching flowers still upon a bit of cloth, although her thread was very coarse these days and the edge of the flowers she made a thing to laugh at for she could not see as once she had, although she would not say she could not, and when the mother found her she said wearily, "What you said was true. I see my maid would be better wed and let it be to that one you know, for I am too weary to look here and there, and always weary somehow nowadays since that flux took me a year or two agone."

Then the old gossip was glad to have something new to do that cost her nothing and she hired a barrow and on it rode the ten miles or so to the valley where her father's house had been and to the village, and there she stayed a day or two and more. On the night when she returned she went to the mother's house and called her out alone to the corner of the house and whispered, "The thing went very well, goodwife, and in a month it can be finished. Well, and I am very weary, too, but still I remember I did it all for you, goodwife, and we are old friends now."

Then the woman took from her bosom a piece of silver she had kept there for this hour and she pressed it on the gossip. But the gossip pushed her hand away and swore she would not have it and it was not needful between two friends and she said this and that but had it in the end.

When all was done and the woman thought it well, or tried to, she told the son's wife, and the son's wife was pleased and showed it, although she took care to say, "You need not have hastened so, mother, for I bear the maid no ill will and she may stay here a year or two for all of me, and I would not mind if it were even all her life, if it were not we are so poor we must count the mouths we feed."

But she was more kindly for the while and she offered of her own will to sew new garments for the maid, three in all, a new coat and trousers of dark blue and some red trousers for her wedding day, as even the poorest maid must have, and besides these a pair of shoes or two, and on the shoes she made a little flower and leaf in red. But they made no great wedding day of it nor any great ado, since the maid was given free and there were no gifts given because she was not good bargain for the man she was to wed.

As for the maid, she said nothing of the day. She listened when her mother told her what was done and she said nothing save once in the night she put out her hand to feel her mother's face near her, and she whispered to her mother suddenly, "Mother, but is it too far for you to come and see me sometimes and how I do there? I am so blind I cannot come to you so far along a road I do not know and over hills and valleys."

Then the mother put out her hand too and she felt the maid trembling and she wept secretly and wiped her tears in the darkness on the quilt and she said over and over, "I will come, my maid, be sure and I will come, and when I come you shall tell me all and if they do not treat you well I will see to it heartily. You shall not be treated ill." And then she said most gently, "But you have lain sleepless all this night."

And the maid answered, "Yes, and every night a while."

"But you need not be afraid, child," the mother answered warmly. "You are the best and quickest blind maid I ever saw, and they know you blind and they cannot blame you for it nor say we hid it from them."

But long after the maid had fallen into light sleep at last the mother lay and blamed herself most heavily, for somehow she felt some wrong within herself that laid its punishment upon the maid, though how she did not know, only she wished she had been better. And she blamed herself lest if by any chance she should have found a nearer place to wed her maid, a village where she could go each month or so, or even found a poor man willing to move to the hamlet for a little price that she could promise. Yet even when she thought of this she groaned within her heart and doubted that her son and son's wife would have spared even this small price, for they kept the money now. So she thought most heavily, "Yet I cannot hope she will never be beaten. Few houses be there like ours where neither man nor his mother will beat a maid new come. And it would tear my heart so, and so grieve me if I saw my blind maid beaten or even if it was done near enough so I could hear of it, or so the maid could run home and tell me, and I helpless once she is wed, that I think I could not bear it. Better far to have her where I cannot see her

and where I cannot know and so be saved the pain because I cannot see and so can hope."

And after she had lain a while more and felt how
heavy life lay on her she thought of one thing she could
do, and it was that she could give the maid some silver
coins for her own, as her own mother had done when she
left home. So in the darkness before dawn she rose and
moving carefully not to stir the beasts and fowls and
frighten them she went to her hole and smoothed away
the earth and took out the bit of rag she kept the little
store in and opened it and chose out five pieces of silver
and thrust them in her bosom and covered the hole
again. Then with the silver in her bosom a little comfort came and she thought to herself, "At least it is not
every maid who comes from a poor house with a little
store of silver. At least my maid has this!"

And holding fast on this small comfort she slept at
last.

Thus the days passed and none joyfully. No, the
woman took no joy even in her youngest son and cared
little whether he came and went except she saw that he
was well and smiling with some business of his own
she did not know. So the day came at last when the
maid must go and the woman waited with the heaviest
heart to see what was the one who came to fetch her.
Yes, she strained her heart to understand what sort of
man it was who came and fetched her maid away.

THE MOTHER

It was a day in early spring he came, before the year had opened fully so that spring was only seen in a few hardy weeds the children in the village digged to eat and in a greenish tinge along the willow twigs and the brown buds on the peach trees scarcely swollen yet. All the lands lay barren still with winter, the wheat not growing yet and but small spears among the clods, and the winds cold.

On this day one came, an old man riding on a gray ass without a saddle and sitting on an old and filthy ragged coat folded under him upon the beast's back. He came to the house where the mother was and gave his name. Her heart stopped then in her bosom, for she did not like the way this old man looked. He grinned at her and shaped his lips to be kind, but there was no kindness in the sharp old fox's face, sharp eyes set in deep wrinkles, a few white hairs about a narrow lipless mouth curved down too long to smile with any truth this day. He wore garments well-nigh rags, too, not patched or clean, and when he came down from his ass there was no common courtesy in his manner, such as any man may have whether he be learned or not. He came limping across the threshing-floor, one leg too short to match the other, his old garments tied about him at the waist, and he said roughly, "I am come to fetch a blind maid. Where is she?"

Then the mother said, for suddenly she hated this old

man, "But what pledge have you that you are the one to have her?"

The old man grinned again and said, "I know that fat goodwife who came to tell us we might have the maid for nothing for my brother's son."

Then the woman said, "Wait until I call her." And she sent her younger lad who lounged about the house that day, and the old gossip came as quickly as her old legs would bear her and she stared at the man and laughed and shouted, "Aye, it is the uncle of the lad she is to wed. How are you, goodman, and have you eaten yet this day?"

"Aye," said the old man grinning and showing all his toothless gums, "but not too well I swear."

All this time the mother looked at him most steadfastly and then she cried out bluntly to the gossip, "I do not like the looks of this! I thought better than this for my maid!"

And the gossip answered loudly laughing, "Goodwife, he is not the bridegroom—his nephew is as soft and mild a lad as ever you did see."

By now the cousin's wife was come too and the son and son's wife and the cousin came and others from the hamlet and they all stood and stared at this old man and it was true that to all he was no good one for looks and ways of any kindness. Yet was the promise given, and there were those who said, "Well, goodwife, you must bear in mind the maid is blind."

And the son's wife said, "The thing is set and promised now, mother, and it is hard now to refuse, for it will bring trouble on us all if you refuse." And when he heard her say this her husband kept his silence.

The woman looked piteously at her cousin then, and he caught her look and turned his eyes away and scratched his head a while, for he did not know what to say. He was a simple good man himself and he did not trust too much this old man's looks either; still it is hard to say sometimes if poverty and evil are the same thing, and it might be his ragged garments made him look so ill, and it was hard to say nay when all the thing was set and done, and so not knowing what to say he said nothing and turned his head away and picked up a small straw and chewed on it.

But the gossip saw her honor was in danger and she said again and again, "But this is not the bridegroom, goodwife," and at last she called, for it would shame her much if the thing were not done now, "Old man, your brother's son is soft as any babe, is he not?"

And the old man grinned and nodded and laughed a meager laugh and said, wheezing as he spoke with laughter, "Aye, soft as any babe he is, goodwife!" And at last he said impatiently, "I must be gone if I am to fetch her home by night!"

So not knowing what else to do, the mother set her maid upon the ass's back at last, the maid garbed in her new garments, and the mother pressed into her hand the little packet of silver and whispered quickly, "This is for your own, my maid, and do not let them have it from you." And as the old man kicked the ass's legs to set it going the mother cried aloud in sudden agony, "I will come, my maid, before many months are past and see how they do treat you there, and keep all in your heart and tell me then. I shall not fear to bring you home again, my maid, if aught is wrong."

Then the blind maid answered through her dry and trembling lips, "Yes, mother, and that cheers me."

But the mother could not let her child go yet and she cast here and there desperately in her mind to think of some last thing to say and hold her yet a little longer, and she cried out to the old man, clinging to her maid, "My maid is not to feed the fire, old man,—she shall not feed the fire, for it hurts her eyes—the smoke—"

The old man turned and stared and when he understood he grinned and said, "Oh, aye, well, let it be so— I'll tell them—" and kicked the beast again and walked beside it as it went.

So the maid went away, and she held her sign of blindness in her hand, and had her little roll of garments tied behind her on the ass's back. The mother stood and watched her go, her heart aching past belief, tears welling from her eyes, and this although she did not know what else she could have done. So she stood still until the hill rose between and cut the child from her sight and she saw her no more.

XVI

NOW must the mother somehow make her days full to ease the fears she had and to forget the emptiness where once the blind maid had sat. Silent the house seemed and silent the street where she could not hear the clear plaintive sound of the small bell her daughter struck whenever she went out. And the mother could not bear it. She went to the land again, against her elder son's will, and when he saw her take her hoe he said, "Mother, you need not work, it shames me to have you work in the field and others see you there when you are aged."

But she said with her old anger, "I am not so aged— let me work to ease myself. Do you not see how I must ease myself?"

Then the man answered in his stubborn way, "To me you seem to grieve for what is not so, my mother, and there is no need to let your heart run ahead into evils that may never come."

But the mother answered with a sort of heavy listlessness that did not leave her nowadays, "You do not understand. You who are young—you understand nothing at all."

THE MOTHER

The young man looked dazed at his mother then, not knowing what she meant, but she would say no more, but went and took a hoe and plodded out across the fields in silence.

But it was true she could not work hard any more, for when she did her sweat poured out, and when the wind blew on her, even a warm wind, it sent a chill upon her and she was soon ill again with her flux. So must she bear her idleness and she worked no more when she was well again, but sat in the doorway idle. There was no need for her to lift her hand about the house, since the son's wife did all and did all well and carefully.

She did all well, the mother thought unwillingly, except she bore no child. The mother sitting empty there looked restlessly about that threshold where once she had been wont to see her little children tumbling in their play, and all day long she sat and remembered the days gone, and how once she had sat so young and filled with life and work, her man there, her babes, she the young wife and another the old mother. Then her man was gone and never heard from—and she winced and turned her mind from that, and then she thought how empty it seemed now, the elder son in the field all day or bickering at harvest with the landlord's agent, some new fellow, a little weazened cousin of the landlord's, people said—she never looked at him—and her blind maid gone, and her younger son gone always in the town and seldom home.

Well, but there was her younger son, and as she sat she thought of him more often, for she loved him still the best of all her children. Into her emptiness he came now and then, and with his coming brought her only brightness. When he came she rose and came out of her bleakness and smiled to see his good looks. He was the fairest child she had, as like his father as a cockerel is like a cock who fathered him, and he came in at ease nowadays, and not fearing his elder brother as once he did, for he had some sort of work in town that brought him in a wage.

Now what this work was he never clearly said, except that it brought him in so well that sometimes he had a heap of money, and sometimes he had none, although he never showed this money to his brother, except in the good clothes he wore. But there were times when he was free and filled with some excitement and then he pressed a bit of silver into his mother's hand secretly and said, "Take it, mother, and use it for yourself."

Then the mother took the silver and praised the lad and loved him, for the elder son never thought to put a bit of money in her hand; since he had been master he kept all his silver for his own. Well fed she always was and she ate heartily as she was able for she loved her food, and better than she had ever been she was with this son's wife to clothe her and make all she needed, and even her burial garments were made and ready for her, though she did not think to die yet for a long time.

Anything she asked for they let her have, a pipe to comfort her, and good shredded tobacco and a sup of yellow wine made hot. But they did not think to put a bit of silver in her hand and say, "Use it for any little thing you wish," and she knew, if she had asked for it the son and his wife would look at each other and say, one or the other of them, "But what would you buy—do we not give you everything?" So when the younger son brought her the bit of silver she loved him for it more than all else the other two did for her, and she kept it in her bosom and when the night came she rose and hid it in the hole.

But still he was not often where she could see him and there upon the empty threshing-floor the two women sat, mother and son's wife, and to the mother it seemed all the house was full of emptiness. She sat and sighed and smoked her pipe and all she had to do these days was to think of her life, or nearly all, for there was that one thing she would not think of willingly, and when she did it brought her blind maid to her mind and she never could be sure the two were not linked somehow in the hands of the gods. Sometimes she would have gone to some temple to seek a comfort of some sort, though what she did not know, but there was the old sin and it seemed late now to seek for forgiveness and she let it be and sighed and spoke of her blind maid sadly sometimes.

But if she did the son's wife answered always sharply,

"She does well, doubtless—a very lucky thing for all that you found one who would have her for his son."

"Now she is a clever maid, too, daughter-in-law," the mother said hotly. "You never would believe how much she could do, I know, but before you came she did much that when you came you would not let her do and so you never knew how well she did."

"Aye, it may be so," said the son's wife, holding nearer to her eyes the cloth she sewed on to see if it were right. "But I am used to working on and finishing with what I do and a blind maid potters so."

The mother sighed again and said, looking over the empty threshold, "I wish you would bear a babe, daughter. A house should have a child or two or three in it. I am not used to such an empty house as this. I wish my little son could wed if you are not to have a child, but he will not, somehow, for some reason."

Now here was the young wife's grief, that though she had been wed near upon five years she had no child yet and not a sign of one, and she had gone secretly to a temple to pray and had done all she knew and still her body stayed as barren as it had been. But she was too proud to show how grieved she was and now she said, calmly, "I will have sons in time, doubtless."

"Aye, but it is time," the mother said pettishly. "I never heard of any women in our hamlet who had not babes if they had husbands. Our men are fathers as soon as they mate themselves and the women always fertile—

good seed, good soil. It must be you have some hidden illness in you somewhere to make you barren and unnatural. I made you those clothes full and big, and what use has it been!"

And to the cousin's wife the mother complained, and she said, leaning to put her mouth against the other's ear, "I know very well what is wrong—there are no heats in that son's wife of mine. She is a pale and yellow thing and one day is like the next and there is never any good flush in her from within, and all your luck in cutting her wedding garments cannot prevail against her coldness."

And the cousin's wife nodded and laughed and said, "It is true enough that such pale and bloodless women are very slow to bear." Then her little laughing eyes grew meaningful and she laughed again and said, "But not every woman can be so full of heats as you were in your time, good sister, and well you know it is not always a good thing in a woman!"

Then the mother answered hastily, "Oh, aye, I know that—" and fell silent for a time and then after a while she said unwillingly, "It is true she is a careful woman, clean and almost too clean and scraping out the pot so often I swear she wastes the food with so much washing of the oil jar and the like. And she washes herself every little time or so, and it may be this is why she goes barren. Too much washing is not always well."

But she spoke no more of heats, for she feared to have

the cousin's wife bring up again that old ill done, although the cousin's wife was the kindest soul and never
all these years had made a difference of it, and if she had
even told her man then the mother never knew she did.
If it had not been for these two sorrows that she had,
the blind maid and that her son had no sons, she might
have forgotten it herself, so far away the days of her
flesh seemed now. Yes, she might have forgotten it if she
had not feared it had been sin and these two sorrows
the punishment for it.

But there her life was, and the maid was blind and
gone now and there was no child, and only the beasts
about and the dog and even these she dared not feed.

There was only this good thing nowadays, she thought,
and it was that her two sons did not quarrel so much.
The elder was satisfied and master in the house, and the
younger had his own place somewhere, and when he
came home and went away again, the most the elder son
did was to say with feeble scorn, "I wonder where my
brother gets those good clothes he wears and what the
work is that he does. I cannot wear clothes like his and I
work bitterly. He seems to have money somehow. I hope
he is not in some band of town thieves or something that
will drag us into trouble if he is caught."

Then the mother flew up bravely as she always did
for her little son and she said, "A very good younger
brother, my son, and you should praise him and be glad

he has gone and found a thing to do for himself and not stayed here to share the land with you!"

And the elder son said sneeringly, "Oh, aye, he would do anything I swear to keep from labor on the land."

But the son's wife said nothing. She was pleased these days because the house was all her own and it was naught to her what the young man did, and she did not complain because he bought his clothes elsewhere now and she needed not to make them for him.

So the time went on and spring came and passed and early summer came and still the mother never could forget her maid. One day she sat counting on her fingers the days since that one when she saw the hill cut the maid off from her sight, and it was more than twelve times all the fingers on her hands and then she lost the count, and so she thought sadly, "I must go to her. I have let this old heaviness weigh on me and I ought to have gone before. If she had been a sound maid she would have come by now to pay the visit that wives do to their old homes, and I could have asked her how she did and felt her hands and arms and cheeks and seen the color of her face."

And the mother sat and looked at those hills around and saw how the summer came on to its full height and every hillside was green and all the grain high in the fields, and she forced her body that was weary always now even though she was idle all the livelong day, and she thought, "I must go and see my maid and I will go at once, seeing I am not needed on the land and here I sit idle. I will go and before the great heat comes, lest my flux drop on me again unaware. Yes—I will go this very tomorrow since there is no sign of cloud in this fair sky—this blue sky—" she looked up at the sky and saw how blue it was and remembered suddenly as she did nowadays some bit of her life long gone, and she remembered the blue robe her man had bought once and that he wore away and she sighed and thought with some dim old pang, "On such a day as this he bought the robe and we quarreled—on just such a fair day, for I remember the robe was the color of the sky that day." She sighed and rose to drive the thought away and when her elder son came she said restlessly, "I think to go and see your sister tomorrow, and how she does in the house where she was wed, seeing she cannot come to me."

Then the son said, anxiously, "Mother, I cannot go with you now, for there is work to do tomorrow. Wait until the harvest is over and the grain threshed and measured, and I have a little free time."

But suddenly the mother could not wait. There was strength in her a plenty yet when she had something she set her mind to do, and she was weary of her idleness and sitting and she said, "No, I will go tomorrow!"

And the son said, worried still and he was always easily worried if aught came that was sudden and out of the common and he could not think what to do quickly, "But how will you go, mother?"

She said, "Why, I will ride my cousin's ass if he will lend it, and do you bid a lad of his to go and call your brother to walk beside and lead the ass, and we will go safe enough, the two of us, for there are no robbers near these days that I have heard tell of, except that new kind in the town they call the communists, who do not harm the poor, they say—"

At last the son was willing, though not too easily and not until his wife said quietly, "It is true I cannot see any great danger if the younger one goes with her."

So they let the mother have her way at last, and the cousin's lad was sent to town to search until he found the younger son and so he did and came back wide-eyed and said, "My cousin and your second son will come, aunt." And then he thought a while and twisted the button on his coat and said again, "I swear it is a strange and secret place where he lives and a hard place to find. He lives in a long room full of beds, some twenty beds or so above a shop, and the room is filled with books and papers. But he does not work in the shop for I asked him. I did not know my cousin could read, aunt. If he reads those books he must be very learned."

"He cannot read," the mother said astonished. "He never told me that he lived by books, a very strange odd thing, I swear! I must ask him of it."

The next day when she was on the ass and they went

winding through the valleys she took the chance of being alone with him and she did ask her son, "What are those books and papers that my cousin's son says you have in that room where you all live? You never told me you could read or that you live by books. I never saw you read a word, my son."

Then the young man stopped the little song he had been singing as they went for he had a good voice to sing and loved to sing, and he said, "Aye, I have learned a little." And when she pressed him further he said, evading her, "Mother, do not ask me now, for some day you will know everything and when the hour comes. A great day, mother, and I was singing of it just now, a song we sing together where I work, and on that day we shall all be eased, and there shall be no more rich and no more poor and all of us shall have the same."

Now this was the wildest talk the mother had ever heard, for well she knew heaven wills who shall be rich and who shall be poor, and men have naught to say but take their destiny and bear it, and she cried out afraid, "I hope you are not in some wicked company, my son, not with thieves or some such company! It sounds the way robbers talk, my son! There is no other way for poor to be rich than that, and it is ill to be rich and lose your life if you be caught at it!"

But the young man grew angry at this and said, "Mother, you do not understand at all! I am sworn to silence now, but some day you shall know. Yes, I shall not forget you on that day. But only you. I will not share with any who have not shared with me." This last he said so loudly that she knew he felt against his brother and so she was silent for a while, fearing to rouse his wrath.

But she could not let him be. She sat as bid upon the ass and clung to the beast's hairy skin and thought about this son and looked at him secretly. There he walked ahead of her, the beast's halter in his hand, and now he was singing again, some song she had never heard, some beating fiery song whose words she could not catch, and she thought to herself that she must know more of his life. Yes, and she must bind him somehow more closely to his home and to them all. She would wed him and have his wife there in the house. Then would he often come and even live there, perhaps, for the wife's sake. She would seek and find a pretty, touching maid whom he could love, for the elder son's wife could do the work, and she would find another sort for this son. And as she thought of this her heart was eased because it seemed a good way and she could not keep it back and so she said, "Son, you are more than twenty now, and near to twenty-one, and I think to wed you soon. How is that for a merry thing?"

But who can tell what a young man's heart will be? Instead of smiling silence, half pleased and half ashamed, he stopped and turned and said to her most wilfully, "I have been waiting for you to say some such thing—

it is all that mothers' heads run upon, I do believe! My comrades tell me it is the chiefest thing their parents say —wed—wed—wed! Well then, mother, I will not wed! And if you wed me against my will, then shall you never see my face again! I never will come home again!"

He turned and went on more quickly and she dared not say a word, but only sat amazed and frightened at his anger and that he did not sing again.

Yet she forgot all this now in what was to come. The path along which they had come since early dawn grew narrower and more narrow toward noon, and those hills which around their own valleys were so gently shaped, so mild in their round curves against the sky and so green with grass and bamboo, rose now as they went among them into sharper, bolder lines. At last when noon was full and the sun poured its heat down straight the gentle hills were gone, and in their place rose a range of mountains bare and rocky and cruelly pointed against the sky. They seemed the sharper too because the sky that day was so cloudless, bright and hard and blue, above the sand color of the bare mountains.

Beneath great pale cliffs the path wound, the stones not black and dark, but pale as light in hue and very strange, and nothing grew there, for there was no water anywhere. So the path wound up and yet more up and when noon was passed an hour or two, they came suddenly into a round deep valley in the mountain tops, and there some water was, for there was a small square village enclosed about with a rocky wall, and about it the green of a few fields. But when the mother and her son stopped at the gate to that village and asked of the place they sought, one who stood there pointed yet higher to a ridge and said, "There where the green ends on that lower edge there are the two houses. It is the last edge of green, and above it there are only rocks and sky."

Now all this time the mother had stared astonished at these mountains and at their strange wild shapes and paleness, and at the scanty green. She had spent her life in the midst of valleys, and now as the path wound up from the enclosed village she stared about aghast to see how mortally poor the land was here and how shallow on the pale rocks the soil was and how scanty all the crops, even now when harvest drew on, and she cried out to the youth, "I do not like the looks of this place, son! I doubt it is too hard a place for your sister. Well, we will take her home, then. Yes, if it is too hard for her here I can walk and we will put her on the ass, and let them say what they will. They paid nothing for her, and I will ask nothing but her back again."

But the young man did not answer. He was weary and hungry, for they had eaten but a bit of cold food they had brought with them, and he longed to reach his sister's house, for there they thought to spend the night. He pulled at the ass's bridle until the mother could not bear it and was about to brave his anger and reprove him.

THE MOTHER

Suddenly they came upon that house. Yes, there the two houses were, caught upon the side of the ridge and stuck there somehow to the rocks, and the mother knew this was where her maid was, for there the ill-looking old man stood at the door of one of the two houses, and when he saw her he stared as if he could not believe it was she, and then he ran in and out came more people, another man, dark and lean and wild in looks, and two women and a slack-hung youth, but not her blind maid.

The mother came down from her ass then and went near, and all these stared at her in silence, and she looked back and was afraid. Never had she seen such looks as these, the women's hair uncombed and full of burrs and their faces withered and blackened with the sun, their garments never washed, and so were they all. They gathered there and out of the other house came a sickly child or two, yellowed with some fever, their lips parched and broken, and their bodies foul with filth, and they all stared silently, and gave no greeting, their eyes as wild and reasonless as beasts' eyes are.

Then did the mother's heart break suddenly with fear and she ran forward crying, "Where is my maid? Where have you hid my maid?" And she ran into their midst, but the young man stood doubting and holding to the ass.

Then a woman spoke sullenly, and her speech was not easily understood, some rude northern speech it was, and the sounds caught between her broken teeth and nothing came out clear and she said, "You have come well, goodwife. She has just died today."

"Died!" the mother whispered and said no more. Her heart stopped, her breath was gone, she had no voice. But she pushed into the nearest hut and there upon a bed of reeds thrown on the ground her blind maid lay. Aye, there the maid was lying quietly and dead, dressed in the same clothes she had when she left her home, but not clean now nor mended. Of those new things there was no trace, for the room was empty save for the heap of rushes and a rude stool or two.

Then the mother ran and knelt beside her maid and stared down at the still face and sunken eyes and at the patient little mouth and all the face she knew so well. And suddenly she burst out crying and she fell upon the maid and seized her hands and pushed the ragged sleeves back and looked at her little arms and drew the trousers up her legs and looked to see if they were bruised or beaten or harmed in any way.

But there was nothing. No, the maid's soft skin was all unbroken, the slender bones whole, and there was nothing to be seen. She was pale and piteously thin, but she was thin always and death is pale. Then did the mother stoop and smell at the child's lips to see if there was any smell of poison, but there was no smell, nothing now except the faint sad scent of death.

Yet somehow the mother could not believe that this was any good and usual death. She turned on those who stood about the door watching her in silence, and she looked at them and saw their wild rude faces, not one of which she knew, and she shouted at them through sudden great weeping, "You have killed her—well I know you have—if you did not, then tell me how did my maid die so soon, and she left me sound and well!"

Then the evil old man whom she had hated from the first time she saw him grinned and said, "Be careful how you speak, goodwife! It is not a small thing to say we killed her and—"

But the sullen, rough-haired woman broke in screaming, "How did she die? She died of a cold she caught, being so puny, and that is how she died!" And she spat upon the ground and said again, screeching as she said, "A useless maid she was, too, if there was one, and knowing nothing—no, she could not even learn to fetch the water from the spring and not stumble and fall or lose her way!"

Then the mother looked and saw a narrow stony path leading down the mountain to a small pool and she groaned and cried, "Is that the way you mean?" But no one answered her and she cried out in further agony, "You beat her—doubtless every day my maid was beaten!"

But the woman answered quickly, "Search and see if there be bruises on her! Once my son did beat her for she came to him too slowly, but that is all!"

The mother looked up then and said faintly, "Where is

your son?" And they pushed him forward, that son they had, and there he stood, a gangling, staring lad, and the mother saw he was nearly witless.

Then did the mother lay her head down upon her dead maid and weep and weep most wildly, and more wildly still she wept when she thought of what the maid had suffered, must have suffered, at such hands as these. And while she wept the anger grew about her in those who watched her. At last she felt a touch upon her and looking up she saw it was her son, and he bent and whispered to her urgently, "Mother, we are in danger here— I am afraid—we must not stay. Mother, she is dead now and what more can you do? But they look so evil I do not know what they will do to us. Come and let us hasten to the village and buy a little food and then press on home tonight!"

The mother rose then unwillingly, but as she looked she saw it was true those people stood together close, and there was that about them to make her fear, too, and she did not like their muttering nor the looks they cast at her and at the youth. Yes, she must think of him. Let them kill her if they would, but there was her son.

She turned and looked down once more at her dead maid and put her garments neat and laid her hands to her side. She went out into the late afternoon. When they saw her calmer and that she made ready to mount the ass again, the man, who had not spoken yet, and who was father to the witless son, said, "Look you, goodwife, if you do not think us honest folk, look at the coffin we have bought your child. Ten pieces of silver did it cost us, and all we had, and do you think we would have bought a coffin if we had not valued her?"

The mother looked then, and there beside the door a coffin truly was, but well she knew there were not ten pieces of silver in it, for it was but the rudest box of unpainted board, and thin well-nigh as paper and such a box as any pauper has. She opened her lips to make angry answer and to say, "That box? But my maid's own silver that I gave her would have paid for that!"

But she did not say the words. It came upon her like a chill cloud across the day that she had need to fear these people. Yes, these two evil men, these wild women —but there her son was tugging at her sleeve to hasten her and so she answered steadily, "I will say nothing now. The maid is dead and not all the angers in the world nor any words can bring her back again." She paused and looked at this one and at that and then she said again, "Before heaven do you stand and all the gods, and let them judge you, whatever you have done!"

She looked at this one and that, but no one answered, and she turned then and climbed upon the ass and the son made haste and led the ass down the rocky path and turned shivering to see if they were followed and he said, "I shall not rest until we are near that village once again and where many people are, I am so fearful."

But the mother answered nothing. What need to answer anything? Her maid was dead.

XVII

CRAZED with her weariness was the mother when she came down from the halting gray ass that night before her own door. She had wept all the way home, now aloud and now softly, and the young man had been beside himself again and again with his mother's weeping. He cried out in an agony at last, "Cease your wailing, mother, or I shall not be able to bear it!"

But when she calmed herself a little for his sake she broke forth again and at last the young man ground his teeth together and he muttered wildly, "If the day were come, if we were not so miserably poor, if the poor were given their share and could defend themselves, then might we sue for my sister's life! But what use when we are so poor and there is no justice in the land?"

And the mother sobbed out, "It is true there is no use in going to law since we have no money to pay our way in to justice," and then she wept afresh and cried, "But all the money and the justice under heaven would not bring my blind maid back again."

At last the young man wept too, not so much for his

sister nor even for his mother, but because he was so footsore and so worn and his world awry.

Thus they came at last to their own door and when she was down from the ass the mother called her elder son piercingly and so sharply that he came running out and she cried, "Son, your sister is dead!" And while he stared at her scarcely comprehending, she poured out the tale, and at the sound of her voice others came quickly to hear the tale until there in the dusk of night nearly all the hamlet stood to hear it. The younger son stood there half fainting, leaning on the ass, and when his mother talked on he went and threw himself upon the ground and lay there dazed with what had come about this day, and he lay silent while his mother wept and cried aloud and in her weeping said, looking with her streaming eyes to this face and to that, "There my little maid was, dead and gone, and I hate myself I ever let her go, and I would not have let her go if it had not been for this cold-hearted son's wife of mine who begrudged the little maid a bit of meat and a little flower on her shoe and so I was fearful if I died and the maid was afraid, too—a little tender child who never would have left me of her own will! What cared she for man or marriage and a child's heart in her always, clinging to her home and me? Oh, son, it is your wife who has brought this on me—I curse the day she came and no wonder she is childless with so hard a heart!"

So on and on the mother cried and at first they all

listened in silence or exclaiming something when they had pieced the tale from what she said between her weeping, and then they tried to comfort her, but she would not let herself be comforted. The eldest son said nothing but stood with downcast head until she cursed his wife and spoke against her child-bearing, and then he said in a reasonable and quiet voice, "No, mother, she did not bid you send my sister to that place. You sent her so quickly and did not say a word to anyone but fixed it so and we wondered even that you did not go and see how it was there for yourself," and he turned to his father's cousin and he said, "Did you not think so, cousin? Do you remember how I said we were surprised my mother was so quick in the matter?"

And the cousin turned his eyes away and muttered unwillingly, chewing a bit of straw, "Oh, aye, a little quick," and his wife who stood holding a grandchild in her arms said mournfully to the mother, "Yes, it is true, sister, you be a very quick woman always, and never asking anyone if this or that is well to be done. No, before any of us know it or guess what it is you are about you have done all and it is finished, and you only want us to say you have done well. It is your nature all your life to be like this."

But the mother could not bear blame this night and she cried out in anger, and so turned her working angry face upon her cousin's wife, "You—you are used to that slow man of yours, and if we must be all judged too quick by such as he—"

And it looked for a time as though these two women who had been friends all their lives would fall to bitter words now, except that the cousin was so good and peaceable a man that when he saw his wife's great face grow red and that she was gathering up her wits to make a very biting answer he called out, "Let be, mother of my sons! She is sore with sorrow tonight and well beside herself." And after he had chewed a while upon his straw, he added mildly, "It is true that I am a very slow man and I have heard it many times since I was born, and you have told me so, too, mother of my sons. . . . Aye, I be slow." And he looked around upon his neighbors and one called out earnestly, "Aye, goodman, you are a very slow-moving man for sure, and slow in wits and slow to speak!"

"Aye," said the cousin sighing a little and spitting out the shattered straw he chewed and plucking out a fresh one from the stack of rice straw near which he stood.

So was the quarrel averted. But the mother was not eased and suddenly her eye fell on the old gossip standing in the crowd, her mouth ajar and eyes staring and all her old hanging face listening to what went on. Seeing her the mother's anger and pain broke out afresh and it all came out mingled with her agony and she rushed at the gossip and fell on her and tore at her large

256

fat face and snatched at her hair and screamed at her and said, "Yes, and you knew what those folk were and you knew the son was witless, and you never said a word of it but told a tale of how they were plain country folk like us, and you never said my maid must go up and down that rocky path to fetch water for them all— it is all on you and I swear I shall not rest myself until I have made you pay for it somehow—"

And she belabored the gossip who was no match for the distraught mother even at the best of times and there is no knowing how it might have come about at the end if the son had not flown to part them and if the younger son had not risen too and with his elder brother held their mother so that the old gossip could make haste away, although she must needs stand, too, for honor's sake when she had gone a distance and far enough so there were those who stood between them, and then she stopped and cried, "Yes, but your maid was blind and what proper man would have her? I did you a very good turn, goodwife, and here be all the thanks I get for it." And she beat her own breast and pointed to the scratches on her face and fell to weeping and working herself up for a better quarrel.

But the crowd hastened her away, and the sons urged the mother into the house and they forced her gently in and led her there, she weeping still. But she was spent at last and let them lead her to her room, and when she was come and they had sat her down, the son's wife fetched her a bowl of water very hot and soothing and she had been heating it while the quarrel went on. Now she dipped a towel in it and wiped the mother's face and hands and poured hot tea out and set food ready.

Then little by little the mother let herself be calmed and she wept more silently and sighed a while and drank a little tea and supped her food and at last she looked about and said, "Where is my little son?"

The young man came forward then and she saw how deathly pale he was and weary and all his merry looks gone for the time, and she pressed him down beside her on the bench and held his hand and urged him to eat and rest himself and she said, "Sleep here beside me to-night, my little son, and on the pallet where your sister used to lie. I cannot have it empty this night, my son." And so the lad did and he slept heavily the moment that he laid himself down.

But even when the house was quiet the mother could not sleep for long. She was spent to her core, her body spent with the long ride and all her heart's weariness, and the only thing that comforted her was to hear the lad's deep breathing as he lay there. And she thought of him then with new love and thought, "I must do more for him. He is the last I have. I must wed him and we will build a new room on the house. He shall have a room for himself and his woman, and then when children come—yes, I must find a good, lusty wife for him so that somehow we shall have children in the house."

THE MOTHER

And this thought of little children yet to come was the only comfort she could see in her whole life ahead of her.

But doubtless even this comfort might not have lasted except that her old flux laid hold on her again and made her weak as death, too weak to mourn. She lay there on her bed for many days, purged body and heart, and all her sorrow and her comfort too in abeyance because she was not strong enough to mourn or hope. Many there were who came to exhort her, her neighbors and her cousin's wife and they said, "Goodwife, after all the child was blind," and they said, "Goodwife, what heaven has made for us we cannot change and it is useless to mourn for anything in this life." And they said, "Remember your good sons," and one day when the cousin's wife said this the mother answered faintly, "Yes, but my elder son's wife she does not bear, and my younger son he will not wed." And the cousin's wife answered heartily, "Give the elder son's wife a year or two, cousin, for sometimes when seven years are passed barren, a woman will come to her true nature and bear a harvest of good children, for I have seen it so, and as for the lad's saying he will not wed, why then he has a love somewhere, and we must find out who she is, and if she is fit for him to wed or not. Yes, truly has he found a love, as young folks will these days, for never was there a man in all the world, I swear, who would not wed!"

But the mother whispered, "Bend down your ear, sister, and put it against my lips," and when the cousin's wife had done this the mother whispered, "Since sorrow follows me and everything goes wrong with me, I fear sometimes it is that old sin of mine that the gods know about—perhaps heaven will not give me grandsons!" And when she thought of this she closed her eyes and two great tears came out from under her closed lids. She thought of all her sins, not only the one the cousin's wife knew of, but all the many times she had said she was widow and the letters that she wrote and all the lies. Not that she held the lies pure sin, since all must lie a little now and then for honor's sake, but here the sin was, that she had lied and said her man was dead. Almost was it now when she thought of it as if she had put her hand forth and brought his death on him, and she had used this lie of death to hope another man would have her. So all these sins of hers, so old she could forget them many days together when she was well, came back fresh and now when she was weak and sorrowful, the heavier because she could not tell them all but must carry them in herself, and heaviest because she was a woman held in good repute among her fellows.

She grew so low in mind that nothing cheered her much except to have her younger son about her. Yes, although the elder son's wife tended her most carefully and brought her food ready and hot when she would have it and even walked a mile or two to another village to fetch a certain sort of dried curd they made there from beans, and although the mother leaned on her in every sort of way and called to her if she would so much as turn herself in her bed, yet the son's wife was no comfort to her, and often when she did her most careful best the mother would scold her that her hands were cold or her face so yellow and stare at her in some half hostile, childish way. But still the older woman never blamed the son's wife any more that she was childless. No, she said no more of that, believing somehow dimly that her own sins might be the cause.

But she rose from her bed at last, and when the autumn was well gone the sharpness of her pain had ebbed with it and she was dreary all day long but not frantic, and she could think of her maid, but the edge of pain was gone. At last she even said to her own heart, "Aye, perhaps even what they say is true, perhaps it is better that my maid is dead. There are so many things worse than death."

And she held fast to this one thought.

And all the hamlet helped her. No one ever spoke of the maid again before her, nor doubtless anywhere, since there is nothing to be remembered in a blind maid and there are many like her everywhere. First they did not speak of her where the mother was, to spare the mother pain, and then they did not speak because there was naught new to tell of it, and because other news came of other things and people, and the maid's little life was ended.

For a while the gossip went carefully where the mother was and took thought not to be alone with her, but when she saw how feeble the mother was when she rose up from her bed, she grew cheerful then and called out greeting as she ever had.

And the mother let the past be silent, except sometimes in her own heart.

XVIII

THEN did it seem as though the mother's heart might have some comfort, for in the springtime of that year the younger son came home and he said, "I am come home to stay a while, mother, how long I do not know, but at least until I am bid to go again."

But when she rejoiced he made little answer and scarcely seemed himself. He was so quiet, never singing or playing his capers or talking in any reckless way as he was used to do, that the mother's heart wondered if he might be ill or troubled with some secret thing. But when she spoke this fear to the cousin's wife that one said, mildly, "Well, it may be he is passing out of his childhood. How many are his years, now? The same I think as my fifth child, and she is twenty now and nearly twenty-one and wed four years. Yes, twenty-one is out of childhood, and men should not caper then as once they did, although I remember that man of yours could caper even to that last day I saw him."

"Aye," said the mother, sighing. Very dim in her now was the memory of the man, and mingled somehow with this younger son of hers, and sometimes when she remembered she could not think how her man had looked alone, because the son's face rose there in his stead.

But at the end of nine days the younger son went as quickly as he came and almost secretly, though how he had his message he must go none knew. But go he did, putting his few garments in a little leathern box he had. His mother grieved to see him go and cried, "I thought you were come to stay, my son," but the son replied, "Oh, I shall be back again, my mother," and he seemed secretly gay again somehow, and eager to be gone.

Thereafter was he always gay. He came and went without warning. He would come in perhaps one day, his roll of clothing under his arm and there he was. And for a day or two he would idle about the little hamlet and sit in the teashop and make great talk of how ill the times were and how uneven justice was and how some great day all this would be made better, and men listened staring at each other, not knowing what to make of it, and the innkeeper scratched his greasy head and cried, "I do swear it sounds like robbers' talk to me, neighbors!" But for the mother's sake and for the good elder son's sake they let him be, thinking him but childish still and to be wiser when he was wed and had a man's life.

Yet when he came home this younger son still sat idle, or else he made as if to help his brother at some light task, although when he did this the brother said scornfully always, "I thank you, brother, but I am used to doing work without you."

Then the youth looked at him in his impudent way, for he grew a very impudent eye these last days, and he would not quarrel but he laughed coolly and he said, and spat in the dust while he said it, "As you will, my elder brother," and he was so cool his elder brother well-nigh burst with hatred of him and gladly would have told him to stay away forever except that a man may not tell his brother this and still be righteous in his neighbors' eyes.

But the mother saw no fault in him at all. Even when he talked his big talk with her and said against his elder brother, "I swear these little landowners that must even rent before they can live, these little men, they are so small and proud that they deserve what shall befall them one day when all the land is made common and no one may have it for his own."

The mother understood no word of this except the first and she said plaintively, "Aye, I do think, too, your brother is over proud sometimes, and his wife barren, too."

For everything this younger son said seemed wise to the mother, now she clung to him so fast. To her when he came home it made a festival, and she would have made each day that he was there a holiday if she could have done it and would have killed a fowl for him and made better food than usual. But this she could not do.

The fowls were her elder son's now, and she could not do better than to steal an egg or two from some nest she found and keep them for her younger son, and when he came pour them into boiling water secretly for him to sup and add to the dish a little sugar that she had saved somehow.

It came to be that whenever any little dainty fell to her or if she went into a house in the hamlet for a visit with a neighbor, since she was so idle now in her age and nothing she must do, and if someone gave her a peach or a dried persimmon or a little cake or some such thing for kindness, she saved it for her younger son. Much time she spent in watching these small bits to see they did not mold, and she kept them as long as she could, and when he put off coming home and she was forced to eat them lest they spoil she felt it no pleasure and scarcely could she enjoy the dainty, although she loved food, too. Often would she open the drawer she kept them in and turn the little store over with her fingers and think to herself, "He does not come. He is not here. If I had a little grandson I could give them to him when my son does not come. I have no one, if my son does not come."

And many hours of each day she sat and looked down the road to catch a glimpse of him as he came and when she saw the glint of a man's robe she would run forward as best she could and when she saw it was her son come home she took his warm smooth hand in her old dry one and she pulled him into her own room and poured out for him the tea the careful son's wife kept there for her and then with pleasure would she bring out the little store she had for him. And she sat down and watched him lovingly while he picked about among the bits and chose the best. Sometimes he turned his dainty nose aside and said, "That cake is mildewed, mother," or he said, "I never liked a rice flour cake so dry."

Then she would answer sorrowfully, "Is it too dry, my son? Well, and I thought you would still like it maybe," and when he would not have it she ate it up herself to keep from wasting it, grieving that it was not good enough for him.

Then when he had eaten what he wished she sat to hear what he would say. Never would he answer all her questions freely as she wished he would and when she pressed him closely he seemed to be in haste to go away, and when she saw this was so, she learned to ask him nothing and he learned, too, to put her off. For as she grew older she forgot more easily and was put off more easily too, and to put her off he would tell her of some wonder he had seen, a juggler who would let a snake crawl down his throat and pull it up again by the tail, or a woman who had borne a two-headed child that she showed for a penny to those who wished to see it, or some such strange sight as may be seen in any town.

And the old mother was diverted by his talk and cried when he was gone, and she could not keep from telling

267

of these wonders to the son and his wife. Once when
she did so the elder son was bent over an earthen bowl
of water, washing off his face after labor in the fields,
and he looked up, his face wet, and said most bitterly,
"Aye, he does not feed you nor do aught else for you
but throw a bit of a coin to you as to a beggar. He comes
here and eats and never puts his hand to hoe or plough
and tells these tales and he is more to you than—" and
he bent his face again and made a noise about his washing and would not listen to what his mother had to say
in answer.

But this was all she knew of her younger son. She
knew his lithe and pretty body, and she knew the pale
gold of his skin, the hue a city man is and different from
the dark and ruddy brown of country folk, and she knew
how the nails grew long upon his two little fingers,
and she knew his teeth were white and his black hair
oiled and shining, and she knew how he let his hair grow
long about his ears and how he tossed his head to keep
his eyes clear of the glossy hair.

Yes, and she knew and loved his ready smile and his
bold eyes and she loved his carelessness with silver and
how he would reach into his girdle and give her what he
had or if he had none ask of her what she had, and more
than to have him give to her she loved to take what she
had and press it on him. All he gave her she saved to
give it back again when he might want it. It was the
best use she knew for her small store.

XIX

BUT one day he did not come when he said he would. And how did she know he would surely come? Because but three days before he had come secretly and by night, walking across the field paths and not through the village, and he scratched lightly on her door, so she was half afraid to open it, thinking it might be robbers. Even as she was about to call out she heard his voice low and quick and luckily the fowls stirred by her bed where they roosted and hid it from the hearing of the elder son and his wife.

She rose then as fast as she could, fumbling her clothes and feeling for the candle, and when she opened the door softly, for she knew it must be for a secret thing he came at such an hour and in such a way, there he was with two other young men, all dressed in the same way he went dressed these days, in black. They had a great bundle of something tied up in paper and rope and when she opened the door with the light in her hand, her son blew the light out for there was a faint moon, enough to see by, and when she cried out but still softly in her pleasure to see him, he said in a whisper, "Mother, there is something of my own I must put under your bed among the winter garments there. Say nothing of it, for I do not want anyone to know it is there. I will come and fetch it again."

Her heart misgave her somehow when she heard this and she opened her eyes and said soberly, holding her voice low as his, "Son, it is not an ill thing, I hope—I hope you have not taken something that is not yours."

But he answered hastily, "No, no, mother, nothing robbed, I swear. It is some sheepskins I had the chance to buy cheap, but my brother will blame me for them for he blames me for everything, and I have nowhere to put them. I bought them very cheap and you shall have one next winter, mother, for a coat—we will all wear good clothes next winter!"

She was mightily pleased then and trusted him when he said they were not robbed and it was a joy to her to share a little secret with this son of hers and she said hastily, "Oh, aye, trust me, son! There be many things in this room that my son and son's wife do not know."

Then the two men brought the bundle in and they pushed it silently under the bed, and the fowls cackled and stared and the buffalo woke and began to chew its cud.

But the son would not stay at all, and when the mother saw his haste she wondered but she said, "Be sure I will keep them safe, my son, but ought they not to be aired and sunned against the moth?"

To this he answered carelessly, "It is but for a day or

two, for we are moving to a larger place and then I shall have a room of my own and plenty."

When she heard this talk of much room, there was that thought in her mind she had always of his marriage, and she drew him aside somewhat from the other two and looked at him beseechingly. It was the one thing about him that did not please her, that he was not willing for her to wed him, because she well knew what hot blood was and there was sign in this son of her own heat when she was young, and she knew he must sate it somehow and she grudged the waste. Better if he were wed to some clean maid and she could have her grandsons. Now even in the haste of the moment when he was eager to be gone, and the other two waiting in the shadows by the door, even now she laid her hand on his hand and she said coaxingly, her voice still whispering, "But, son, if you have so much room, then why not let me find a maid? I will find the best pretty maid I can —or if you know one, then tell me and let me ask my cousin's wife to be the one to make the match. I would not force you, son, if it be the one you like is one that I would like too."

But the young man shook his long locks from his eyes and looked toward the door, and tried to shift her hand away. But she held him fast and coaxed again, "Why should your good heats be spent on wild weeds here and there, my son, and give me no good grandsons? Your brother's wife is so cold I think there will never be chil-

dren on my knees unless you put them there. Aye, you
are like your own father, and well I know what he was.
Plant your seeds in your own land, my son, and reap the
harvests for your own house!"

But the young man laughed silently and tossed his
hair back again from those glittering eyes of his and said
half wondering, "Old women like you, mother, think of
nothing but weddings and births of children, and we—
we young ones nowadays have cast away all that. . . .
In three days, mother!"

He pulled himself away then and was gone, walking
with the other two across the dimly lighted fields.

But three days passed and he did not come. And three
more came and went and yet three more, and the mother
grew afraid and wondered if some ill had come upon her
son. But now in this last year she had not gone easily
to the town and so she waited, peevish with all who
came near her, not daring to tell what her fears were,
and not daring either to leave her room far lest her son's
careful wife chance to draw the curtains aside and see
the bundle under her bed.

One night as she lay sleepless with her wondering she
rose and lit the candle and stooped and peered under the
bed, holding the parted curtains with one hand. There
the thing was, wrapped in thick paper, shaped large and
square and tied fast with hempen rope. She pressed it
and felt of it and there was something hard within, not
sheepskin surely.

THE MOTHER

"It should be taken out to sun, if it is sheepskin," she muttered, sore at the thought of waste if the moth should creep in and gnaw good skins. But she did not dare to open it and so she let it be. And still her son did not come.

So passed the days until a month was gone and she was near beside herself and would have been completely so, except that something came to wean her mind somewhat from her fears. It was the last thing she dreamed of nowadays and it was that her son's wife conceived.

Yes, after all these cool years the woman came to herself and did her duty. The elder son went to his mother importantly one day as she sat in the doorway and said, his lean face all wrinkled with his smiles, "Mother, you shall have a grandson."

She came out of the heavy muse in which she spent her days now and stared at him out of eyes grown a little filmy and said peevishly, "You speak like a fool. Your wife is cold as any stone and as barren and where my little son is I do not know and he scatters his good seed anywhere and will not wed and save it."

Then the elder son coughed and said plainly, "Your son's wife has conceived."

At first the mother would not believe it. She looked at this elder son of hers and then she shouted, pulling at her staff to raise herself upon her feet, "She has not—I never will believe it!"

But she saw by his face that it was true and she rose

and went as fast as she could and found her son's wife who was chopping leeks in the kitchen and she peered at the young woman and she cried, "Have you something in you then at last?"

The wife nodded and went on with her work, her pale face spotted with dull red, and then the mother knew it to be true. She said, "How long have you known?"

"Two moons and more," the young wife answered.

Then the old mother fell into a rage to think she was not told and she cried, striking her staff against the earthen floor, "Why have you said no word to me, who have sat all these years panting and pining and thirsting for such news? Two moons—was ever so cold a soul as you and would not any other woman have told the thing the first day that she knew it!"

Then the young woman stayed her knife and she said in her careful way, "I did not lest I might be wrong and grieve you worse than if I never gave you hope."

But this the mother would not grant and she spat and said, "Well and with all the children I have had could not I have told you whether you were right or wrong? No, you think I am a child and foolish with my age. I know what you think—yes, you show it with every step you make."

But the young woman answered nothing. She pressed her lips together, those full pale lips, and poured a bowl of tea from an earthen pot that stood there on the table and she led the mother to her usual place against the wall.

But the mother could not sit and hold such news as this. No, she must go and tell her cousin and her cousin's wife and there they sat at home, for nowadays the sons did the work, the three who stayed upon the land, the others having gone elsewhere to earn their food, and the cousin still did what he could and he was always busy at some small task or other. But even he could not work as he once had, and as for his wife, she slept peacefully all day long except when she woke to heed some grandchild's cry.

And now the mother went across the way and woke her ruthlessly and shouted at her as she slept, "You shall not be the only grandmother, I swear! A few months and I am to have a grandson too!"

The cousin's wife came to herself then slowly, smiling and licking her lips that were grown dry with sleeping, and she opened her little placid eyes and said, "Is it so, cousin, and is your little son to be wed?"

The mother's heart sank a little, and she said, "No, not that," and then the cousin looked up from where he sat, a little weazened man upon a low bamboo stool, and he sat there twisting ropes of straw for silkworms to spin cocoons upon, since it was the season when they spin, and he said in his spare dry way, "Your son's wife, then, cousin?"

"Aye," the mother said heartily, her pleasure back

again, and she sat down to pour it out, but she would not seem too pleased either, and she hid her pleasure with complaints and said, "Time, too, and I have waited these eight years and if I had been rich I would have fetched another woman for him, but I thought my younger son should have his chance before I gave his brother two, and marriage costs so much these days even for a second woman, if she be decent and not from some evil place. A very slow woman always that son's wife of mine, and full of some temper not like mine—cold as any serpent's temper it is."

"But not evil, goodwife," said the cousin justly. "She has done well and carefully always. You have the ducks and drakes now that you did not used to have upon the pond, and she mated that old buffalo you had and got this young one, and your fowls are twice as many as you had and you must have ten or twelve by now, besides all the many ones sold every year."

"No, not evil," said the mother grudgingly, "but I wish she could have used heats other than the heats of beasts and fowls."

Then the cousin's wife spoke kindly but always full of sleep these days, and she said, yawning as she spoke, "Aye, she is different from you, cousin, to be sure—a full hot woman have you always been and one to do so much, and still hearty. Why, when you walk about, if you have not your flux, I do wonder how you walk so quick. I do

276

marvel, for if I must walk from bench to table and from table to bed, it is as much as I can do these days."

And the cousin said admiringly, "Aye, and I cannot eat half what I used to do, but I see you sitting there and shouting for your bowl to be filled again and then again."

And the mother said modestly but pleased at all this praise, "Oh, aye, I eat as well as ever. Three bowls and often four I eat, and I can eat anything not too hard since my front teeth fell away, and I am very sound at such times as I have not got my flux."

"A very sound old soul," murmured the cousin's wife, and then she slept a little and woke again and saw the mother there and smiled her wide sleepy smile and said, "A grandson, did you say? Aye, we have seven now of grandsons alone—and none too many—" and slept again peacefully.

So did the great news fill the days that had been empty because the younger son did not come, and this new joy took the edge from the mother's waiting and she thought he must come some time or other and let it rest at that.

But it was not all joy either, and like every joy she ever had, the mother thought, there was always something wrong in it to make it go amiss if so it could. Here the thing was. She feared lest the child be born a girl and when she thought of this she muttered, "Yes, and it would be like my ever evil destiny if it were born a girl."

And in her anxiety she would have liked to go and ask that potent little goddess that she knew and make a bribe to her of a new robe of red or new shoes or some such thing if she would make the child a boy. But she did not dare to go lest she recall to the goddess' mind that old sin of hers, and she feared the goddess lest her old sin was not yet atoned for, even with the sorrow that she had, and that if the goddess saw her and heard her speak of grandsons, she might remember and reach out and smite the little one in the womb. She thought to herself, most miserably, "Better if I do not go and show myself at all. If I stay away and do not tell her that the child is coming, she may forget me this long time I have not been to any gods, and it will be but the birth of another mortal and not my grandson, and I must chance it is a boy."

And then she grew uneasy and full of gloom and thought to herself that if the child were joy yet was it a new gate for sorrow to enter by, too, and so is every child, and when she thought of this and how the child might be born dead or shapen wrong or dull or blind or a girl or any of these things, she hated gods and goddesses who have such powers to mar a mortal, and she muttered, "Have I not been more than punished for any little sin I did? Who could have thought the gods would know what I did that day? But doubtless that old god in the shrine smelled the sin about him and told the goddess somehow even though I covered up his eyes.

Well, I will stay away from gods, so sinful an old soul as I be, for even if I would I do not know how to atone more for what I did than I have atoned. I swear if they measured up the joy and sorrow I have had in my whole life the sorrow would sink the scales like stone, and the joy be nothing more than thistledown, such poor joys as I have had. I did not bear the child and I have seen my blind maid die, still blind. Does not sorrow atone? Aye, I have been very full of sorrows all my life long, always poor too, with all my sorrows. But gods know no justice."

So, she thought gloomily, she had two sorrows to bear now: fear lest her grandson be not whole and sound or else a girl, and waiting for this younger son who would not come. Sometimes she thought her whole life was only made of waiting now. So had she waited for her man to come who never came, and now her son and grandsons. Such was her life and poor stuff it was, she thought.

Yet she must hope and whenever anyone went into town she always asked him when he came back again, "Saw you my little son today anywhere?" And she would go about the hamlet and to this house and that and say, "Who went to town today?" And when one said he had, she asked again, "Saw you my little son today, goodman?"

All through the hamlet in those days of waiting the men and women grew used to this question and when they looked up and saw her leaning on the staff her son had cut for her from a branch of their own trees and heard her old quavering voice ask, "Neighbor, saw you my little son today?" they would answer kindly enough, "No, no, good mother, and how could we see him in the common market-place where we go and he such as he is, and one you say who lives by books?"

Then she would turn away dashed of her hope again and she let her voice sink and mutter, "I do not know—well and I think it is he has to do with books somewhere," and they would laugh and say to humor her, "If some day we pass a place where books are sold we will look in and see if he is there behind the counter."

So she must go home to wait and wonder if the moths had eaten up the sheepskins.

But one day after many moons there came news. The mother sat by the door as ever she did now, her long pipe in her fingers, for she had only just eaten her morning meal. She sat and marked how sharply the morning sun rose over the rounded hills and waited for it hoping for its heat, for these autumn mornings were chill. Then came suddenly across the threshold a son of her cousin's, the eldest son, and he went to her own elder son who stood binding the thong of his sandal that had broken as he put it on, and he said something in a low voice.

She wondered even then for she had seen this man start for the town that morning when she rose at dawn, since she could not lie abed easily if she were well, being used to dawn rising all her life, and she saw him start to town with loads of new-cut grass. Here he was back so soon, and she was about to call out and ask him if he had sold his grass so quick when she saw her elder son look up from the thong and cry aghast, "My brother?"

Yes, the old mother's sharp ears heard it, for she was not deaf at all and she called out quickly, "What of my little son?"

But the two men talked on earnestly and very gravely and with anxious looks into each other's faces and at last the mother could not bear it and she rose and hobbled to them and she struck her staff upon the beaten earth and cried out, "Tell me of my son!"

But the cousin's son went away without a word and the elder son said, halting, "Mother, there is something wrong. I do not know—but, mother, I must go to town and see and tell you then—"

But the mother would not let him go. She laid hold on him and cried out the more, "You shall not go until you tell me!"

And at the sound of such a voice the son's wife came and stood and listened and said, "Tell her, else she will be ill with anger."

So the son said slowly, "My cousin said—he said he saw my brother this morning among many others, and his hands were tied behind him with hempen ropes and his clothes were rags and he was marching past the market-place where my cousin had taken the grass to sell, and there was a long line of some twenty or thirty, and when my brother saw him he turned his eyes away —but my cousin asked and the guards who walked along said they were communists sent to gaol to be killed to-morrow."

Then did the three stare at each other, and as they stared the old mother's jaw began to tremble and she looked from this face to the other and said, "I have heard that word, but I do not know what it is."

And the son said slowly, "So I asked my cousin and he asked the guard and the guard laughed and he said it was a new sort of robber they had nowadays."

Then the mother thought of that bundle hid so long beneath her bed and she began to wail aloud and threw her coat over her head and sobbed and said, "I might have known that night—oh, that bundle underneath my bed is what he robbed!"

But the son and son's wife laid hold on her at this and looked about and hurried her between them into the house and said, "What do you mean, our mother?"

And the son's wife lifted up the curtain and looked at the man and he came and the old mother pointed to the bundle there and sobbed, "I do not know what is in it—but he brought it here one night—and bade me be secret for a day or two—and still he is not come—and never came—"

Then the man rose and went and shut the door softly

and barred it and the woman hung a garment over the window and together they drew that bundle forth and untied the ropes.

"Sheepskins, he said it was," the mother murmured, staring at it.

But the two said nothing and believed nothing that she said. It might be anything and half they expected it was gold when they felt how heavy and how hard it was.

But when they opened it, it was only books. Many, many books were there, all small and blackly printed, and many sheets of paper, some pictured with the strangest sights of blood and death and giants beating little men or hewing them with knives. And when they saw these books, the three gaped at each other, all at a loss to know what this could mean and why any man should steal and hide mere paper marked with ink.

But however much they stared they could not know the meaning. None could read a word, nor scarcely know the meaning of the pictures except that they were of bloody things, men stabbed and dying, and men severed in pieces and all such bloody hateful things as happen only where robbers are.

Then were the three in terror, the mother for her son and the other two for themselves lest any should know that these were there. The man said, "Tie them up again and let them be till night and then we will take them to the kitchen and burn them all."

But the woman was more careful and she said, "No,

we cannot burn them all at once or else others will see the mighty smoke and wonder what we do. I must burn them bit by bit and day by day as though I burned the grass to cook our food."

But the old mother did not heed this. She only knew now that her son had fallen in evil hands and she said to her elder son, "Oh, son, what will you do for your little brother—how will you find him?"

"I know where he is," the man said slowly and unwillingly. "My cousin said they took them to a certain gaol near the south gate where the beheading ground is."

And then he cried out at his mother's sudden ghastly look and he called to his wife and they lifted the old woman and laid her on the bed and there she lay and gasped, her face the hue of clay with terror for her son, and she whispered gasping, "Oh, son, will you not go— your brother—"

And the elder son laid aside his fears for himself then slowly and he said, in pity for his mother, "Oh, aye, mother, I go—I go—"

He changed his clothes then and put shoes on his feet and to the mother the time went so slow she could not bear it. When at last he was ready she called him to her and pulled his head down and whispered in his ear, "Son, do not spare money. If he be truly in the gaol, there must be money spent to get him out. But money can do it, son. Whoever heard of any gaol that would not let a man free for money? Son, I have a little—in a hole here—I only kept it for him—use it all—use all we have—"

The man's face did not change and he looked at his wife and she looked at him and he said, "I will spare all I can, my mother, for your sake."

But she cried, "What does it matter for me?—I am old and ready to die. It is for his sake."

But the man was gone, and he went to fetch his cousin who had seen the sight and the two went toward the town.

What could the mother do then except to wait again? Yet this was the bitterest waiting of her life. She could not lie upon her bed and yet she was faint if she rose. At last the son's wife grew frightened to see how the old woman looked and how she stared and muttered and clapped her hands against her lean thighs and so she went and fetched the old cousin and the cousin's wife, and the pair came over soberly and the three old people sat together.

It was true it did comfort the mother somewhat to have the others there, for these were the two she could speak most to and she wept and said again and again, "If I have sinned have I not had sorrow enough?" And she said, "If I have sinned why do I not die myself and let it be an end of it? Why should this one and that be taken from me, and doubtless my grandson, too? No, I shall never see my grandson. I know I never shall, and it will not be I who must die." And then she grew angry at such sorrow and cried out in her anger, weeping as she cried, "But where is any perfect woman and who is without any sin, and why should I have all the sorrow?"

Then the cousin's wife said hastily, for she feared that this old mother might cry out too much in her pain, "Be sure we all have sins and if we must be judged by sins then none of us would have children. Look at my sons and grandsons, and yet I am a wicked old soul, too, and I never go near a temple and I never have and when a nun used to come and cry out that I should learn the way to heaven, why then I was too busy with the babes, and now when I am old and they come and tell me I must learn the way before it is too late, why then I say I am too old to learn anything now and must do without a heaven if they will not have me as I am."

So she comforted the distraught mother, and the cousin said in his turn, "Wait, good cousin, until we hear what the news is. It may be you need not grieve after all, for he may be set free with the money they have to free him with, or it may be my son saw wrong and it was not your son who went past bound."

But the cousin's wife took this care. She bade the young wife go and see to something or other in her own house, for she would have this son's wife out of earshot, lest this poor old woman tell more than she meant to tell in this hour, and a great pity after keeping silence so many years.

THE MOTHER

So they waited for the two men to return and it was easier waiting three than one.

But night drew on before the mother saw them coming. She had dragged herself from her bed and as the afternoon wore on she went and sat under the willow tree, her cousin and her cousin's wife beside her, and there the old three sat staring down the hamlet street, except when the cousin's wife slept her little sleeps that not even sorrow could keep from her.

At last when the sun was nearly set the mother saw them coming. She rose and leaned upon her staff and shaded her eyes against the golden evening sun and she cried, "It is they!" and hobbled down the street. So loud had been her cry, so fast her footsteps, that everyone came out of his house, for in the hamlet they all knew the tale but did not dare to come openly to the mother's house, for fear there might be some judgment come on it because of this younger son and they all be caught in it. All day then they had gone about their business, eaten through with curiosity, but fearful too, as country people are when gaols and governors are talked of. Now they came forth and hung about, but at a distance, and watched what might befall. The cousin rose too and went behind the mother, and even the cousin's wife would fain have come except now she did not walk unless she must and she thought to herself that she would hear it but a little later and she was one who believed the best must happen after all and so she spared herself and sat upon her bench and waited.

But the mother ran and laid hold on her son's arm and cried out, "What of my little son?"

But even as she asked the question, even as her old eyes searched the faces of the two men, she knew that ill was written there. The two men looked at each other and at last the son said soberly, "He is in gaol, mother." The two men looked at each other again and the cousin's son scratched his head for a while and looked away and seemed foolish and as though he did not know what to say, and so the son spoke again, "Mother, I doubt he can be saved. He and twenty more are set for death and in the morning."

"Death?" the mother shrieked, and again she shrieked, "Death!"

And she would have fallen if they had not caught her.

Then the two men led her in to the nearest house and put a seat beneath her and eased her down and she began to weep and cry as a child does, her old mouth quivering and her tears running down and she beat her dried breasts with her clenched hands and cried out, accusing her son, "Then you did not offer them enough money—I told you I had that little store—not so little either, forty pieces of silver and the two little pieces he gave me last—and there they are waiting!" And when she saw her son stand with hanging head and the sweat bursting out on his lip and brow she spat at him in her anger and she said, "You shall not have a penny of it either! If he dies it will not be for you. No, I will go and throw it in the river first."

Then the cousin's son spoke up in defense and for the sake of peace and he said, his face wrinkling in such a distressful hour and cause, "No, aunt, do not blame him. He offered more than twice your store. He offered a hundred pieces for his brother, and to high and low in that gaol, as high as he could get he offered bribes. To this one and to that he showed silver, but they would not even let him see your little son."

"Then he did not offer enough," the mother shouted. "Whoever heard of guards in a gaol who are not to be bribed? But I will go and fetch that money this moment. Yes, I will dig it up and take it, old as I am, and find my little son and bring him home and he shall never leave me more, whatever they may say."

Again the two men looked at each other and the son's face begged his cousin to speak again for him and so the cousin's son said again, "Good aunt, they will not even let you see him. They would not let us in at all, I say; no, although we showed silver, because they said the governor was hot now against such crime as his. It is some new crime nowadays, and very heinous."

"My son has never done a crime," the mother cried proudly, and she lifted up her staff and shook it at the man. "There is an enemy somewhere here who pays more than we have to keep him in the gaol." And she looked around about the crowd that stood there gaping now and drinking down the news they heard, their eyes staring and their jaws agape, and she cried at them, "Saw any of you any crime my little son ever did?"

This one looked at that and each looked everywhere and said no word and the mother saw their dubious looks and somehow her heart broke. She fell into her weeping again and cried at them, "Oh, you hated him because he was so fair to look upon—better than your black sons, who are only hinds—aye, you hate anyone who is better than yourselves—" and she rose and staggered forth and went home weeping most bitterly.

But when she was come home again and they were alone and none near except the cousin and the cousin's wife and their children, the mother wiped her eyes and said to her elder son more quietly yet in a fever, too, "But this is letting good time pass. Tell me all, for we may save him yet. We have the night. What was his true crime? We will take all we have and save him yet."

There passed between the son and son's wife a look at this, not evil, but as though forbearance were very near its end in them, and then the son began, "I do not know what the crime is rightly, but they call him what I told you, a communist. A new word—I have heard it often, and when I asked what it was it seemed to be a sort of robber band. I asked the guard there at the gaol, who stands with a gun across his arm, and he answered, 'What is he? Why, one who would even take your land from you, goodman, for himself, and one who contrives against the state and so must die with all his fellows.' Aye, that is his crime."

The mother listened hard to this, the candle's light falling on her face that glistened with dried tears, and she said astounded, her voice trembling while she strove to make it firm, "But I do not think it can be so. I never heard him say a word like this. I never heard of such a crime. To kill a man, to rob a house, to let a parent starve, these be crimes. But how can land be robbed? Can he roll it up like cloth and take it away with him and hide it somewhere?"

"I do not know, mother," said the son, his head hanging, his hands hanging loose between his knees as he sat upon a little stool. He wore his one robe still, but he had tucked the edge into his girdle, for he was not used to robes, and now he put it in more firmly and then he said slowly, "I do not know what else was said, a great deal here and there in the town we heard, because so many are to be killed tomorrow and they make a holiday. What else was said, my cousin?"

Then the cousin's son scratched his chin and swallowed hard and stared at the faces round about him in the room and he said, "There was a great deal said by those town folk, but I dared not ask much for when I asked more closely what the pother was about the guards at the gaol turned on me and said, 'Are you one of them, too? What is it then to you if they are killed?' And I

291

dared not say I was the cousin of one to be killed. But we did find a chief gaoler and we gave him some money and begged for a private place to speak in and he led us to a corner of the gaol behind his own house and we told him we were honest country folk and had a little poor land and rented more, and that there was one among the doomed to die who was a distant relative, and if we could save him then we would for honor's sake, since none of our name had died under a headsman's blade before. But only if it did not cost too much since we were poor. The gaoler took the silver then and asked how the lad looked and we told him and he said, 'I think I know the lad you mean, for he has been very ill at ease in gaol, and I think he would say all he knows, except there is a maid beside him bold as any I have ever seen who keeps him brave. Yes, some are hard and bold and do not care however they may die or when they die. But that lad is afraid. I doubt he knows what he has done or why he dies, for he looks a simple country lad they have used for their bidding and made great promises to him. I believe his crime is that he was found with certain books upon him that he gave among the people freely, and in the books are evil things said of overturning all the state and sharing all the money and the land alike.'"

Then the mother looked at her elder son and broke out in fresh weeping and she moaned, "I knew we ought to let him have some land. We might have rented a little more and given him a share—but no, this elder son of mine and his wife must hold it all and grudge him everything—"

Then the elder son opened his mouth to speak, but the old cousin said quietly, "Do not speak, my son. Let your mother blame you and ease herself. We all know what you are and what your brother was and how ill he hated any labor on the land or any labor anywhere."

So the son held his peace. At last the cousin's son said on, "We asked the gaoler then how much silver it would take to set the lad free, and the gaoler shook his head and said that if the lad were high of place and son of some great rich and mighty man then doubtless silver used could set him free. But being a country lad and poor no man would put his life in danger for all that we could give, and so doubtless he must die."

At this the mother shrieked, "And shall he die because he is my son and I am poor? We have that land we own and we will sell it to free him. Yes, we will sell it this very night,—there are those in this hamlet—"

But the elder son spoke up at this talk of his land and he said, "And how then will we live? We can scarcely live even as it is and if we rent more and at these new and ruinous rates we have now we shall be beggars. All we own is this small parcel of land and I will not sell it, mother. No, the land is mine—I will not sell it."

And when he said this his wife spoke up, to say the only thing she had said all the time, for she had sat there

quietly listening, her pale face grave and showing nothing and she said, "There is the son I have in me to think
of now."

And the man said heavily, "Aye, it is he I think of."

Then was the old mother silent. Yes, she was silent
and she wept a while and thereafter all that night whenever fresh words broke forth there was but this one
answer to them all.

When the dim dawn came near, for they had sat the
night through, the mother gathered some strange
strength she had and said, "I will go myself. Once more
I will go into the town and wait to see my little son if
he must go out to die." And they laid their hands upon
her arm and begged her not to go, and the son said earnestly, "Mother, I will go and fetch him—afterwards—
for if you see the sight you yourself will die." But she
said, "What if I die?"

She washed her face and combed the bit of gray hair
left on her head and put a clean coat on herself as ever
she was used to do when she went townwards, and she
said simply, "Go and fetch my cousin's ass. You will
let me have it, cousin?"

"Oh, aye," the cousin said helplessly and sadly.

So the son and cousin's son went and fetched the ass
and set the old mother on its back and they walked to
the town beside it, a lantern in the son's hand, for dawn
was still too faint to walk by.

THE MOTHER

Now was the mother weak and quiet and washed by her tears, and she went almost not knowing what she did, but clinging to the ass's back. Her head hung down and she did not look once to see the dawn. She stared down into the pale dusty road that scarcely showed yet through the darkness. The men were silent, too, at that grave hour, and so they went winding with the road to the south and entered in toward the southern gate that was not opened yet as they came because the day was still so early.

But there were many waiting there, for it had been noised about the countryside that there would be this great beheading and many came to see it for a show and brought their children. As soon as the gates were opened they all pressed in, the mother on her ass, and the two men, and they all turned to that piece of ground near the city wall within a certain open space. There in the early morning light a great crowd stood already, thick and pressed and silent with the thought of this vast spectacle of death. Little children clung hard to their parents in nameless fear of what they did not know, and babes cried out and were hushed and the crowd was silent, waiting hungrily, relishing in some strange way and hating, too, the horror that they craved to see.

But the mother and the two men did not stay in the crowd. No, the mother whispered, "Let us go to the door of the gaol and stand there," for in her poor heart she still held the hope that somehow when she saw her son some miracle must happen, some way must come whereby she could save him.

So the man turned the ass's head toward the gaol and there it was, and beside its gate set in the high wall spiked with glass along the top they waited. There a guard stretched himself and by him a lantern burned low, the candle spilling out a heap of melted tallow red as blood, until a chill wind blew up suddenly with the dawn and blew the guttering light out. There the three waited in the dusty street, and the mother came down from the ass and waited, and soon they heard the sound of footsteps stirring, and then the sound of many footsteps made on stone and marching and then there was a shout, "Open the gates!"

The guards sprang up then and stood beside the gates erect, their weapons stiff and hard across their shoulders, and so the gates swung open.

Then did the mother strain her eyes to see her son. There came forth many persons, youth tied to youth and two by two, their hands bound with hempen thongs, and each two tied to the two ahead. At first they seemed all young men, and yet here and there were maids, but hard to tell as maids, because their long hair was shorn and they wore the garments that the men did, and there was nothing to show what they were until one looked close and saw their little breasts and narrow waists, for their faces were as wild and bold as any young man's.

The mother looked at every face, at this one and at

that, and suddenly she saw her own lad. Yes, there he
walked, his head down, and he was tied to a maid, and
his hands fast to hers.

Then the mother rushed forward and fell at his feet
and clasped them and gave one loud cry, "My son!"

She looked up into his face, the palest face, his lips
white and earthen and the eyes dull. When he saw his
mother he turned paler still and would have fallen had
he not been bound to the maid. For this maid pulled at
him and would not let him fall, nor would she let him
stay, and when she saw the old white-haired woman at
his feet she laughed aloud, the boldest, mirthless laugh
and she cried out high and shrill, "Comrade, remember
now you have no mother and no father, nor any dear to
you except our common cause!" And she pulled him on
his way.

Then a guard ran out and picked the mother up and
threw her to one side upon the road and there she lay
in the dust. Then the crowd marched on and out of
sight and to that southern gate, and suddenly a wild song
burst from them and they went singing to their death.

At last the two men came and would have lifted up
the mother, but she would not let them. She lay there in
the dust a while, moaning and listening in a daze to
that strange song, yet knowing nothing, only moaning on.

And yet she could not moan long either, for a guard
came from the gaol gate and prodded her most rudely

with his gun and roared at her, "Off with you, old hag—" and the two men grew afraid and forced the mother to her feet and set her on the ass again and turned homeward slowly. But before they reached the southern gate they paused a while beside a wall and waited.

They waited until they heard a great roar go up, and then the two men looked at each other and at the old mother. But if she heard it or knew what it was, she made no sign. She sat drooping on the beast, and staring into the dust beneath its feet.

Then they went on, having heard the cry, and they met the crowd scattering and shouting this and that. The men said nothing nor did the old mother seem to hear, but some cried out, "A very merry death they died, too, and full of courage! Did you see that young bold maid and how she was singing to the end and when her head rolled off I swear she sang on a second, did she not?"

And some said, "Saw you that lad whose red blood spurted out so far it poured upon the headsman's foot and made him curse?"

And some were laughing and their faces red and some were pale, and as the two men and the mother passed into the city gate, there was a young man there whose face was white as clay and he turned aside and leaned against the wall and vomited.

But if she saw or heard these things the mother said

no word. No, she knew the lad was dead now; dead, and no use silver or anything; no use reproach, even if she could reprove. She longed but for one place and it was to get to her home and search out that old grave and weep there. It came across her heart most bitterly that not even had she any grave of her own dead to weep upon as other women had, and she must go and weep on some old unknown grave to ease her heart. But even this pang passed and she only longed to weep and ease herself.

When she was before their door again she came down from the ass and she said pleading to her elder son, "Take me out behind the hamlet—I must weep a while."

The cousin's wife was there and heard it and she said kindly, shaking her old head and wiping her eyes on her sleeves, "Aye, let the poor soul weep a while—it is the kindest thing—"

And so in silence the son led his mother to the grave and made a smooth place in the grass for her to sit upon and pulled some other grass and made it soft for her. She sat down then and leaned her head upon the grave and looked at him haggardly and said, "Go away and leave me for a while and let me weep." And when he hesitated she said again most passionately, "Leave me, for if I do not weep then I must die!"

So he went away saying, "I will come soon to fetch you, mother," for he was loath to leave her there alone.

Then did the mother sit and watch the idle day grow bright. She watched the sun come fresh and golden over all the land as though no one had died that day. The fields were ripe with late harvest and the grain was full and yellow in the leaf and the yellow sun poured over all the fields. And all the time the mother sat and waited for her sorrow to rise to tears in her and ease her broken heart. She thought of all her life and all her dead and how little there had been of any good to lay hold on in her years, and so her sorrow rose. She let it rise, not angry any more, nor struggling, but letting sorrow come now as it would and she took her measure full of it. She let herself be crushed to the very earth and felt her sorrow fill her, accepting it. And turning her face to the sky she cried in agony, "Is this atonement now? Am I not punished well?"

And then her tears came gushing and she laid her old head upon the grave and bent her face into the weeds and so she wept.

On and on she wept through that bright morning. She remembered every little sorrow and every great one and how her man had quarreled and gone and how there was no little maid to come and call her home from weeping now and how her lad looked tied to that wild maid and so she wept for all her life that day.

But even as she wept her son came running. Yes, he came running over the sun-strewn land and as he ran he beckoned with his arm and shouted something to her but she could not hear it quickly out of all her maze of sorrow. She lifted up her face to hear and then she heard him say, "Mother—mother—" and then she heard him cry, "My son is come—your grandson, mother!"

Yes, she heard that cry of his as clear as any call she ever heard her whole life long. Her tears ceased without her knowing it. She rose and staggered and then went to meet him, crying, "When—when—"

"But now," he shouted laughing. "This very moment born—a son—I never saw a bigger babe and roaring like a lad born a year or two, I swear!"

She laid her hand upon his arm and began to laugh a little, half weeping, too. And leaning on him she hurried her old feet and forgot herself.

Thus the two went to the house and into that room where the new mother lay upon her bed. The room was full of women from the hamlet who had come to hear the news and even that old gossip, the oldest woman of them all now, and very deaf and bent nigh double with her years, she must come too and when she saw the old mother she cackled out, "A lucky woman you are, goodwife—I thought the end of your luck was come, but here it is born again, son's son, I swear, and here be I with nothing but my old carcass for my pains—"

But the old mother said not one word and she saw no one. She went into the room and to the bed and looked down. There the child lay, a boy, and roaring as his

301

father said he did, his mouth wide open, as fair and stout a babe as any she had ever seen. She bent and seized him in her arms and held him and felt him hot and strong against her with new life.

She looked at him from head to foot and laughed and looked again, and at last she searched about the room for the cousin's wife and there the woman was, a little grandchild or two clinging to her, who had come to see the sight. Then when she found the face she sought the old mother held the child for the other one to see and forgetting all the roomful she cried aloud, laughing as she cried, her eyes all swelled with her past weeping, "See, cousin! I doubt I was so full of sin as once I thought I was, cousin—you see my grandson!"

COLOPHON

This is one of the titles in the series of the Oriental Novels of Pearl S. Buck. Other titles include *Dragon Seed, East Wind: West Wind, A House Divided, The House of Earth (trilogy), Imperial Woman, Kinfolk, The Living Reed, Mandala, Pavilion of Women, Peony, The Promise, Sons,* and *The Three Daughters of Madame Liang.*

This book was typeset by Alabama Book Composition, Deatsville, Alabama and printed by Data Reproduction, Auburn Hills, Michigan on acid free paper.